The Power of Life

BY

Anthony J Rockweiler

Anthony J Rockweiler

Anthony J Rockweiler

CONTENTS

I dedicate this book to my Wife who was young herself at the time of this event. Her Love and Compassion saw me through something I will never forget especially when most people wrote me off. She was young herself at the time of this ordeal and her life too changes in a dramatic way that day.

ACKNOWLEDGMENTS

To all the people who played a role in my recovery and touched me in some way or another, you left imprint in my life forever.
To all those who made this book possible I cannot Thank you enough.

Chapter 1

A NEW BEGINNING

The Story I'm about to share with you is a rather unbelievable one, but it is true. I was in an accident when I was thirty-six. At the time I was employed by a large grocery chain and worked in the main warehouse distribution facility. I started with the company when I was twenty years old. I also begin bodybuilding when I was twenty-five. I had no clue at the time just how exercise would play a role in this process and my recovery. As I worked my way up in the company sixteen years would pass. Then, little did I know that on a beautiful Monday afternoon at 12:35 pm my life would never be the same. That day I was in an accident. The accident would be traumatic—life altering. Yet, I would like for you to come away with an understanding that not all situations in life will go our way. We will all come across certain events that we must overcome, and learn to deal with— obstacles if you will. As powerful as this event was, it would end in a gratifying way, because I went on to live a happy and fulfilling life. You can too—even against overwhelming odds.

So sit back and read what appears to be an unbelievable journey that life laid out for me.

In this event, dates, times and years would play a fascinating role as I stepped back and studied them. My destiny and fate collided in such a way that it would leave one wondering, How could that be? I would need to bond with life all over again in order to save my life and create my own miracle— through the miracle of belief. Was this a restart of a new life for me? If so, why. I always felt different for some reason or another throughout my life.

Finding any kind of peace in those days was not easy. The suffering would linger for years until I found the key to unlock the mysteries that lie within each one of us. I would search in a desperate way to find that peace and happiness I once possessed all over again. The odds and conditions I faced were unbelievable. I found myself overwhelmed early on. It became apparent rather quickly that I would need to find that precious key if I were to move forward and recover my life.

When most people saw me back then, they said,

"He's not coming back from that." "Do you see the injuries he sustained?" There were also several other factors involved. Such as the day it happened, along with the time it happened. It led me to believe this was a rather odd set of coincidences—perhaps more like a destiny to fulfill. Perhaps there was an underlying message for me to carry in some way or another.

Here is what I saw as I stood back and viewed the overall picture while writing this story. There were certain dates, times and years that surfaced allowing me to see these occurrences as rather unusual. No one could plan something like that.

The day it happened was May 10ᵗʰ at 12:35 pm. May 10th was also my 16th wedding anniversary. I was also born the tenth child in my family at 12:35 pm. I was also with the company for sixteen years at the time of this ordeal. I was bodybuilding for eleven years at the time of the accident and there are eleven children in my family. The number eleven surfaced several other times also. As I began to study the timing of these occurrences even closer, I could see other dates and years that coincide with this event, even down to the time I was born. I find it rather odd and too coincidental just how this all played out. Only life can write a script like this. As you read on, you too may begin to feel like you're experiencing something remarkable or mystical just as I did. You will get to see first-hand just how powerful the human mind and this universe can be. I had to rely on my belief system in a way I never did before and it set my feet on an unbelievable path as I struggled to regain my life once again.

This event would send me on a journey that I will always remember and test me in ways I will never forget.

This process begins on Monday morning, May 10, 1993. I got up that morning like any other morning, got ready for work, and left my home. The only thing different that day would be the man who left that morning would never return home again. It was after lunch and I would need to go into our twenty-below freezer to look at one of the refrigeration units we were having trouble with that day. This freezer itself was about the size of a large grocery store. It had twelve refrigeration units in it to keep it at twenty below zero. The unit was thirty feet from the concrete floor and above racks where food was stored. While I was in the freezer looking at one of the refrigeration units, someone struck the lift I was on with a loaded forklift causing me to fall thirty feet end over end. By all accounts, it was 12:35 pm. On the way down I struck my forehead on the iron forklift cage. The force spun me to the concrete floor causing other serious injuries. The damage would be extensive and severe. I was unconscious for a few minutes.

As I regained conscious from the fall they could see the damage I sustained within seconds. You could no longer recognize me. The paramedics rushed me to the hospital, knowing I suffered a serious head injury along with other serious complications. Meanwhile, my work called my wife at her job telling her that I was in an accident at work. My wife asked if it was serious and they said, "Yes ... hurry." When she arrived at the hospital the nurse came out to inform her that I suffered a serious head injury. She also stated there were other injuries involved. My wife asked if she could see me. So the nurse took her in the back to see me but I could only imagine what was going through her mind. I was not in any condition or resembled the man that left that morning for work. I could only imagine how afraid she must have been, the uncertainty, the fear, and the unknown. Next, the neurosurgeon came out to speak with my wife to let her know that I would need Neurosurgery right away. They also called in an ENT and an orthopedic surgeon to assist the neurosurgeon and assess the other injuries. The operation would last six hours. The neurosurgeon would need to repair a tear I had on the left side of my brain in an area called the frontal lobe.

The surgeon would also need to repair my olfactory nerves that severed at the time of the accident. Then the ENT stepped in to reconstruct my sinuses and forehead. When the six-hour surgery was over the neurosurgeon came out to speak with my wife once again. He explained to her that he didn't know at the time if I would suffer paralysis on my right side or not. He also mentioned that I could be blind in my left eye because of the damage done to my optical nerve. There were many unanswered questions at the time. The neurosurgeon really did not know if I would survive at all or how I would function if I did. He mentioned that the first twenty-four hours would be critical to my survival. After that my chances of surviving would increase at the forty-eight-and seventy-two hour marks.

It was just a waiting game in those early hours after the surgery.

As time went on I did regain consciousness, but there were still many unanswered questions. The neurosurgeon asked me three specific questions before and after surgery. "Who's the president? What year is it? What hospital are you in? "I was able to answer two of the questions correctly. Who is the president and what year is it. I had no idea where I was. After the surgery they put me in the intensive care unit. At that point my wife went home to check on our kids to make sure they were okay. A young woman herself, would leave, go home and try to explain to them, what happened that Monday at work to their father. They must have been so afraid. I know she never realized it at the time, but she would need to step into my role also as the fight for my life would take some time. I could only imagine what was going through their mind. Once again there was so much uncertainty, will my dad be OK. Will he recover from his injuries? Will he make it? How frighten they must have been. A young woman and two young kids spun off into another world instantly to deal with their own uncertainty and fear. This emotional roller-coaster would be just that. I could only imagine. After speaking with the kids, she called the ICU at the Hospital to see how I was doing. The nurse said to her that I regained consciousness to a degree. The nurse tried to put the phone to my ear, but I must have somehow motioned that no one was there. At that point, she spoke with my wife for a second and then put the phone back to my ear once again. I again motioned to her that no one was there. That's when they realized I was completely deaf in my right ear.

As I regained consciousness, a different person would emerge. This would set my feet on a path that would lead me on an unbelievable journey through life. This journey would test how strong I would need to be in order to survive and regain my life. The injuries I sustained were extensive. Before the accident I was an engineer and a bodybuilder. I thought of myself as a bright fellow and resourceful throughout my life. All those traits I once cherished vanished in an instant. I was no longer that person.

My forehead on the left side along with my left jaw muscle would need surgery to repair the damage done from the fall. I suffered a tear on the left side of my brain that would need surgery. I was completely deaf in my right ear and I lost fifty percent of my hearing in my left ear. My olfactory nerves severed from the fall and would need to be reattached. As a result the neurosurgeon said I would never taste or smell again. Another situation I needed to deal with was the muscles around my left eye. The damage affecting that area would cause me to have double vision and leave my vision itself poor. The injury also left me with a fifth-grade reading and a seventh-grade mathematic capability.

All three of my attention spans were altered in the fall—my focused, my divided, and my alternating attention. My short-term memory along with damage to my left jaw would also be affected.

My left foot fractured in three places along with some tissue damage to my ankle. My right knee would suffer damage along with my left shoulder. I also had issues that affected my neck and back. The area around my nose and front teeth were numb from the impact for about three months.

A few months later the neurosurgeon said that he had no idea what would return or what would not. It appeared as though my identity slipped away from me that day in May, all in a split second. Speaking words took a tremendous amount of energy and effort—and simple words at that. I could not articulate words or carry sentences well at all. Reaching for words to form sentences became difficult and frustrating. My once good vocabulary diminished, frustrating me even more. Migraine headaches were almost a daily ordeal. It appeared as if I lost all my strength and I was weak all the time. I did not realize it at the time, but I would need to go on and build a new personality and a new person all over again. My life didn't slow down that day, it came to a complete stop. The man I once knew slipped away.

The world I once remembered was no longer the world I lived in. It drove me inward, into my mind, isolating me from the world I once loved. I found myself consumed by my circumstances day and night. The first year I spent eight hours a day in therapy. Then I would spend years trying to recover what I lost in a split second. I had no clue just how long it would take to recover my life.

The neurosurgeon thought I might be blind in my

left eye due to the optic nerve damage, but, fortunately, once I regained consciousness I was able to see. Only my vision was blurry and I could not see far. In addition, the muscles around my left eye were affected which left me with double vision.

After returning home, every day I would wake up and stand in front of the mirror exercising my eyes. I'm not sure why I did it, I just did. If I would turn my face to the right about halfway, I could see one of everything. If I turned my head straight, my eyesight would begin to double. Therefore, each morning I would perform this exercise by rotating my head back and forth for about 10 to 15 minutes exercising my eyes. I remember using my earlobe as a reference point as I watched the image of my face split in the mirror as I turned. That was something my instincts told me to do. Throughout this ordeal I learned to trust my instincts like never before as they led me into another world.

With many of my five senses diminished I had to rely a great deal on that voice inside of me that I never knew existed. At times, it was as if someone else stepped in and was beginning to help me. I did this daily until my eyesight began to improve with each passing day. I would say it took me about four months of exercising my eyes to bring my eyesight back in alignment once again. My vision itself was poor, but it began to improve over the same course of time. When I think about some of the resources I needed to use in order to rehab myself, it still amazes me.

THE NOISE

When I think of this the word "intrusive" definitely comes to my mind. The psychological effect of this alone was tremendous and crushing. There were times early where I had no clue what was going on. This brings in a completely new and different type of suffering. "One day you are somebody, and in a split second, you are somebody else." I know this condition alone would test me in ways I could never imagine and leave me wondering, "could I survive".

You see three or four months had passed since the accident and I was home alone one day. Everything was quiet at the time. It was just me, no television, no noise, just complete silence. Then I begin to hear a faint noise in my right ear. It was my hearing beginning to return. At first, it was low and sounded like something off in the distance, far away. I didn't know what to think or what was taking place, I thought I might be going crazy. I was so confused and lost at the time. I found myself daily trying to cope and stay alive. I never realized exactly what was taking place. It was just a mass of confusion. I remember as each day passed that noise began to get louder and louder. That condition terrified me and became extremely dangerous. The noise got so loud over the course of a few weeks it was like standing beside a freight train. It scared me knowing that there was no escape and there was no way to turn it off. I realized there was nowhere to go. It kept driving me further inward as time went on, isolating me even more from the world I once knew, and loved. I found myself standing on the edge of reality many days. I did not know what to do or what to think. There were days where I had no idea how I would get by or survive. I really didn't.

That noise brought a completely new and different dimension of suffering into play. I also knew there was no way of escaping it. I could not turn it off and knowing that made it even worse. In the first couple of years I can remember the psychological effect and the toll it took on me. I just kept thinking of a way I could escape that noise, but it just seemed so limited. My physician tried different medications to suppress it, but they had little effect. I can remember not knowing where to turn. Just what were my options? After peeling everything away, it came down to just two alternatives—whether I wanted to live or die. I found myself clinging to life, wanting to live, even in a desperate situation. If I was going to survive I needed some type of quality of life. At least what I perceived to be a decent quality of life.

This was not like the physical pain and suffering. This was a conflict between you and your mind. It became a chaotic state between sanity and insanity. Until you experience something like this, you just never know. The noise would drive me to the very edge on more than one occasion. This ordeal would prove to be completely different from anything I experienced before. The suffering was relentless. I could see my belief system and my faith tested like never before.

This ordeal pushed me to terrifying and unknown places in my mind, on many occasions. What I mean by terrifying and unknown is this. We all deal with fear and the unknown. However, this carried me to a place in my mind that was unknown to me. Somewhere I've never been to before. The scale of fear and the unknown was off the normal chart for me. Coping was difficult day in and day out with the noise. The other medical conditions I was dealing with would only compound the situation even more. This nightmare would also be more complicated than anything I experienced in my life before. This tested me in ways unimaginable. My belief would need to be stronger than ever if I was going to survive. I always believed in myself. However, my belief in myself and my belief that something would change would need to be on a much deeper level. A completely new scale if you will. If I was going to survive, I had to believe in things I once thought were impossible. I also did what my instincts told me to do early on, which was sleep. That way I could try to escape the suffering and buy some time to cope. Therefore, I slept a great deal the first two years after the accident hoping to adapt which helped me get by to some degree. When I was not in therapy I was sleeping.

The migraine headaches, depression, and anxiety were all taking their toll on me. Being in therapy every day for eight hours with that noise was daunting. It took me a long time to be able to deal with that condition. I spent a lot of time meditating and going deep within my mind to find peace and a safe place of refuge time after time. Coexisting with the noise seemed so limited and chaotic I knew something would have to give within myself in order for me to survive.

My old personality wanted everything back the way it was. Yet, I could see that was not going to happen. So as a result, that became part of my agreement with life. I had to think much differently than before. I was trying my best to accept or eradicate every condition I had at the time and move forward. I was juggling so many obstacles at once, but it was difficult. I took one-step forward every day even if it was a small one. Something compelled me each day to push forward. But believe me, there were many days when I felt I could not go on. To me, dealing with all that chaos over a short period is one thing, but over the long haul it becomes a different story. The process begins to wear you down in every way possible, mentally, physically, emotionally and psychologically. You begin to see the world in a different way than you did before. I tried to remember that passion I once had for life and I wondered if it would ever return to me once again. There were many days I thought, will I ever be happy and at peace like before? I had no idea what the outcome would be.

Dealing with these different conditions day in and day out would test my sanity in ways I never knew existed. The noise alone would drive me to a place in my mind where I thought at times, the end could be near. I tried to seek some type of coping mechanism. You are not born with a condition like this and all the sudden it appears out of nowhere and quickly, it's not normal. This noise and the psychological affect it caused would be one of the most difficult challenges I would ever face in my life. I had no idea at the time if I could escape that situation and survive.

You know you wake up one day and suddenly you find yourself in a situation like this. I found myself struggling to survive daily and trying to understand at the same time, "who am I" or who will I be. Part of me knew it was not right, but the other part of me knew there was nothing I could do about it. It was just a lot of emotions I was dealing with that appeared to be out of control or to the extreme at times. In the beginning I couldn't go out around people, once again that fear had a hold on me. It was a fear I never experienced before, holding me prisoner. Even than I can remember how much I wanted to live as I felt caught between two worlds struggling to survive. The world I once remembered and the world where I knew very little. I would force myself to go out to the mall just to be around people and try to get some kind of normalcy back into my life. I would not speak to anyone out of fear, but I just kept going out. I questioned many things—my belief system, my trust in man, and my own being. I know fear can, at least this type of fear, can crush you if you let it. At the time, I didn't know of anyone with the type of injury I was dealing with. Yet something kept me moving forward hanging on to life by a thread.

Three months would pass by before I would undergo a neuropsychological evaluation. This would determine not only the extent of my injuries but also how much therapy I would need. The testing would take thirteen hours to do and give them a blueprint of the problems and medical conditions I was facing. Around the same time I began to see a neuropsychiatrist who would play an instrumental role in my recovery.

From the testing they realized I would need eight hours of therapy every day for the first year. My physicians recommended a hospital nearby. One of the doctors I saw in therapy would be a neuropsychologist who also played a key role in my recovery. Each therapist played a key role in my recovery. This hospital had one of the best programs in the country for treating the type of injury I sustained. Actually, I didn't enter therapy until about eight months after the injury.

The migraine headaches along with that noise made it virtually impossible to function during therapy. I can remember crying many days overcome by my circumstances. I was an independent person my entire life which only made matters more difficult. I remember there were so many major injuries all at one time making it harder to function in therapy. They pulled me inward into my mind like a vacuum, and I could not seem to find my way out, no matter what I did.

I found myself desperate and clinging on to life not knowing where to turn. There were many days when I walked a narrow line between life and death. I hung on to hope as if it was life itself. The doctors called the noise I had in my hearing tinnitus, which they define as a ringing in your ears. The physiological effect from that noise created a completely new and different dimension of suffering. It drew me into a cycle that I could not seem to get out of and kept pulling me further inward each day. To me, if I could not eradicate the noise completely, I had no idea what I was going to do, or if I could move on. The time finally came when I realized it might not go away. That was hard for me to accept and deal with.

The insurance company did not make matters any easier for us to handle. There were many times when they disregarded paying my doctors. They appeared to be cold and unwilling to help. It put a great deal of stress on my family and I, but they did not seem to care. I developed an anger that was unlike any anger I experienced before because of the way they were treating us. I can recall one day telling my doctor that I had to find a way to deal with that anger because I knew it was not helping me. It was not an anger that lashed out, but I realized I needed to let that anger go. I knew in order to move forward that I would need to vent that anger in a positive way allowing me to heal. I mentioned to my physician that I used to have a passion for life and that I based my happiness on living that way. Therefore, from that day forward I came up with a couple of positive affirmations. One of them was, "I want to be at peace and live life with a passion every day like I used to. The other was," Every day in every way I'm getting better and better." So, upon awakening, I would say these affirmations to myself daily as I reinforced them in my mind. My affirmations became part of my everyday routine. I said them until they became an integrated part of my mind on a subconscious level. Second nature if you will. I no longer had to think about the affirmations. They became part of my mind.

At first, nothing appeared to happen. Yet, over the course of time, perhaps a month or two, I can remember waking up one morning and having a smile on my face. It was a rather odd feeling at first because I was wondering what I was smiling about. I knew then that my perception about my circumstances was beginning to change. The way I saw life and the way I saw my situation was beginning to shift. I began to sense there was something taking place that was beyond my understanding. It felt as if this process was beginning to re-mold me into the person I would become. I still had certain conditions affecting me, but the way I began to see them was starting to change. Finding a way to live with them and be happy was a challenge, but something was beginning to alter. My belief and my perception would become a vital part of me surviving. They would allow me to move forward once again. I could see the two molding me together. What was transpiring between this universe and me would alter my life and the way I saw this world forever. My mind was beginning to help me perform certain task that I had no understanding of at the time. I would see something unbelievable taking place as time went on. Seeing this would alter my view of life as I knew it.

This process was molding me along the way into the man I would become. I had no idea what the outcome would be.

There were things taking place inside of me that I did not understand at the time. I was trying my best to control my emotions but it was difficult. At times, I could feel what appeared to be this sensation or feeling of a sixth sense. It was something I could not explain, as if I was tapping into another dimension within my mind. I believe being in such a fragile and altered state at the time forced me to tap into an area of my mind that I could not explain or never new existed. I would come to realize by doing so how it would lead me to a place that would help assist in the healing process and ultimately save my life.

The feeling of being alone would linger on for quite some time. There were many days I wondered, "Who am I" and how will I find my way back to be the person I was before. Will I become someone new or someone different? I was bright, keen, and articulate. Where did all those traits go? Yet, the old part of me knew what happened, but the new part of me was still confused about so many things. I could not spell simple words or form sentences. I was forgetful and lethargic. I had many conditions to put in perspective and the tools were not yet available to me. The one tool that would come into play would be patients in the midst of chaos. I began to get the feeling the universe would provide everything I would need to gain control and save my life. Many of the tools I would seek and find would come in the most unusual way. Yet, they would allow me to find peace and happiness and lead me back to a fulfilling life once again. That is something we all seek. As you follow along you will begin to see how the human mind and words are more powerful than you could ever imagine.

Chapter 2

The Power of Life

I would come to understand just how powerful the term "The Power of Life" would be. I went seeking a place we all have in our mind and came away with a profound understanding of life. I experienced where

"The Power of Life" comes from. That understanding determines who we are as a human being and the quality of the life we live. It defines our connection with life itself.

While meditating one day I would drift deep into my mind to a place where I've never been before to seek peace and healing. Once there, I found the refuge and hope I would need in order to stay alive. I can see how important it was for me to seek refuge at that particular time from all the inflicting conditions. It would set me free from a dark place that I found myself in for so long. In order for me to save my life connecting to a greater power at that time was critical. It was then I knew a power much greater than I could imagine stepped in.

I believe the Creator would grant me a miracle as I returned with my life and was able to move forward once again. I felt what I believe to be the power of life and pure love for the first time. I would meditate many days until the miracle of belief would change my life forever. That day I sensed a presence I knew was much greater than mankind. A presence I believed to be the Creator. After meditating that day my injuries and my life would be much different from before. My perception of all things would change.

Traditional medicine played a vital role in my recovery. Each doctor and therapist carried a special gift for me. I will always be thankful for that. Yet, I would need the power of my mind to turn things around at that time. I would suffer for years, not days, weeks, or even months. So over that period it became crucial that something needed to change and change soon. As I look back now I believe I could see my own miracle, the miracle of belief beginning to unfold. I believe each one of us has that unique ability to heal ourselves and create that miracle. It is the power of belief in conjunction with the Creator when all things become possible.

Belief and the faith we put in it are the pathways to those miracles. "It's your belief in your faith that will heal you." The human mind has so many pathways lying within it just waiting for us to access them. I believe many may never access what I needed to in order for me to live once again. ----------------------

I also believe in western countries no one teaches you how to meditate at an early age so you can reap the benefits of meditation. Yet, on the other hand, anyone can come away with the same results I did by doing what I did. Going within your mind for healing I believe is a universal law of Creation.

Our society focuses on only what you can see and hear. I was fortunate to be able to reach that place in my mind especially at that particular time, it was critical. Every day I would go to what I called, "the place". A place in my mind that I believe we all possess. I went seeking this place and tapped into it in order to find peace and serenity once again. Getting to that place became a little easier and more comfortable with each passing day. As I became more familiar with the man I would become I could also see how this process was recreating me with each passing day. There were things revealed to me that were remarkable then and are still remarkable to me today. Every day in every way I still witness that power. I am living it every moment of every day and I remain amazed by what it did for me then and continues to do for me now. Something seems to flow through me now that I was not aware of before. Life seems to pull me along as if it was suppose to be that way. I believe everyone we meet holds some particular key to our lives in some way or another. I also believe people are instruments of the universe that can further advance our lives. Miracles come in many ways and through many different methods or events.

This process also moved my consciousness to a new level of awareness and each day I seek a higher level.

This experience has allowed me to expand my mind in ways I could never imagine. It seems as though I have lived two or three lifetimes in a relativity short period of time. Life and the suffering process revealed many things to me about living the kind of life I would like to live. As a result, I realize that life is even more precious than ever before. I also view the meaning of life different than before. This does not mean I am perfect by any means. It just means the tools life provided me would help advance my spirit to a new level in the physical world we live in. I seem to be more in harmony with life than ever before and I feel that is not a coincidence or a mistake.

I feel, see, and sense things that I was not aware of before. I also view and see this universe in a different way than before. I have a new connection and a new belief about this world as I created a new life for myself. The power of my mind took me to a place where I made connections to another world or another dimension where a new life would be waiting for me. I am lucky to have made it through this ordeal. I know there is a higher power that governs everything. I feel I was in the process of healing myself whether it was with the doctors at first, or on my own reaching into my mind. Nevertheless, something happened one day that changed everything and I saw and felted my life renewed. I saw my perception of life and the things around me different than before the accident.

I believe by some way or another that we are all

connected. I know we can tap into our minds and find that power that can renew and heal our life. I wake up every morning and say my affirmations each day, which only connects me to life on a deeper level. Each day brings a new beginning along with new people that seem to change my life in some way or another. Each day I cannot wait to see what life has in store for me. I find myself going places and expecting to meet good people and have good experiences. It is such a profound feeling. It's a feeling of authentic power. It also brings me a sense of peace and happiness that I did not have before. I just have the power of belief that this universe, the Creator will always look out for me.

I know there came a point in this process where every day I pictured it to be a beautiful day, a new beginning. Happiness appeared to get better and better with each day. I went out believing good things were going to happen and in return that is what transpired. I just took on this belief that what I thought about would come to me. Meaning if I thought of good things than good things would come. I seem to have a sense that I did not possess before. Almost like a six sense. It brings a feeling of empowerment into my life. I believe when something like this happens to you it puts you on another wavelength or another level of consciousness. You are no longer operating or seeing life or even making decisions as you once did. I seem to meet people in a different way than I did before. When I had to re-learn to use words over once again I also learned to use and choose my words much differently than before. I believe as a result, between my thought process and my ability to use words differently, it drew people into my life that just wanted to help.

It appeared odd at first but I think I was just getting more in harmony with life itself. I realized then how the power of thought and belief was starting to take effect. It appeared to be getting stronger and stronger each day. I could not explain it any other way. I am glad I clung onto hope saying my affirmations daily and using the power of thought over and over which would eventually save my life. Meditating is a powerful force.

I was fortunate in this process to find the hope I would need that would change the course of my life. This was one of the tools provided to me as I begin to realize how powerful my affirmations, just these simple words, would actually be. I could see a new world opening for me as each tool became another asset in molding me into the person I am today. My life would be much different than it was before. As a result, there is an energy coming from me that appears to be different from before. As humans, I believe you can see the energy of life coming off of a person in some way or another.

I know through my own story how your life can change and what could take place just by believing. Your perception of living will begin to shift and life will feel much better than before. It will begin to feel like you are starting over once again. Each day the positive people that come into my world are amazing. It seems like I witness the "power of life" every day, and when I do it makes me feel empowered and humbled. People have often said this to me, "I wish I could meet interesting people in my life every day". I respond by saying, "Look for them in your life. You may not be paying attention. That's all. They are coming into your world. Just be aware of it." If you change your perception you will begin to see them each day. As you start to perceive life in a new way your perception of everything will begin to change. You will begin to see the world in a different way also. Life is just waiting on you for the first move. Life's perception does not need to change.

When I look back now, I can remember in the early stages of this ordeal how I searched for relief. I wondered if I would find that relief from the pain and suffering before time ran out. I was scared and frail in those days. The uncertainty and fear I was experiencing plagued me daily. On many occasions I had no clue what to do or where to turn. However, in those days life still held me in the balance and the Creator embraced me with love and carried me to a new life. I felt my spirit calling on me every day to move to a new level of awareness and accept a new meaning of life itself. Therefore, I continued to search and go deeper and deeper within my mind because something told me to do so.

I stayed on that path until I connected with life on a different level and began to see life in a different way. On one incredible day in my mind I connected to something, a greater power that would change the course of my life. That day transformed who I was as I came away with a miracle and the gift of life. Although I continued to have many problems something changed that day. An encounter would take place causing me to see my life and the obstacles I was dealing with in a different way than before. The world as I knew it began to alter as I returned to a new life. It also began to change my view of this world and my perception of life itself.

The noise I had in my head from my hearing damage was so invasive and terrifying it drove me farther into my mind, isolating me even more. Think about it, when I say the noise. Imagine you are standing beside a train. Imagine you are hearing that every waking moment. There is no walking away. That noise tried it's best to keep me from moving forward. Yet, something about it changed that day—not the noise itself, but the way I begin dealing with it began to change. I began to cope with it in a different way than I did before and view it in more a positive light. I started thinking that the noise was going to have to live with me, rather than I was going to have to live with it. It was still difficult, but I could see a glimmer of hope in my life when I would need it most. I believe life knew that as well. That noise alone subjected me to a suffering that I could not escape. That is not something you prepare yourself for in life. There were many days when I didn't know if I could get past that noise and recover my life. When it entered into play, I was already in a fragile state of mind. So getting a hold on it when I did was crucial in order to save my life. Walking that narrow line between darkness and light in those days taught me a valuable lesson. A lesson I will never forget and one I will always be thankful for, as it humbled me throughout this process. This universe exposed me to something so different, so extreme, yet so compassionate. I can say this now, there was a good thing about being in that deep sorrow I found myself in at the time.

Now it does not take much to make me happy anymore. I wake up many days with a smile on my face feeling grateful to be alive. I believe I connected to a greater power on a spiritual level at a critical time in my life. I also believe my spirit knew how delicate I was at that particular time. It led me to a place in my mind knowing I was at the end of the road and clinging to life by a thread. As my life hung suspended in time, I made that turn which gave me the hope I would need to save my life. I am so thankful that I was able to reach that place and come back with the miracle of life.

You can find this place of peace and serenity too by spending a little time each day meditating in silence. In that silence you will find your spirit waiting to assist you and move you to a new level of awareness. This place in your mind I speak of is where you will find true peace and serenity. You will begin to feel like good things are beginning to happen to you and for you. You and life will begin to feel as one and things will seem to flow in a more natural state.

I also believe that you are what you think and you think what you become. You create your own reality by what you believe. Life already knows that, but we must believe it in order for it to translate into a reality. Have you ever wondered what it would be like if everyone in your life was positive?

The support system you would have would be

phenomenal. We would empower ourselves beyond belief and into a new reality. As humans we are the highest intelligence on earth that can reason. Yet we seem to reason ourselves into despair without being able to find hope once again.

Remember, life is your friend not your enemy. I know we can heal ourselves through thought and influence the outcome by belief. That connection has a profound feeling. Our mind is one of the greatest tools we have at our disposal. When something happens to us there may be things at the time that we just do not understand. Yet over the course of the event we must try to listen because many of the answers lie within us. Life itself is trying to give you the best understanding of what is taking place. Then we can assist, say through meditation and enhance the outcome to heal ourselves. We have areas of our mind that are capable of healing us and all we must do is seek those "places" in our mind. I have come to understand that once something happens, it is over. There is no looking back. You have what you have and got what you got. Moving forward takes center stage and becomes the important part. What becomes vital then is how we approach what happened in a positive way so we can renew our life. Looking at it in a positive light is the only way. Otherwise, nothing else will help you move forward.

I am glad I had positive people around me to give me positive support and feedback when I needed it most. It made a world of difference to me. Find those positive people in your life that can give you that support when you need it most. Surround yourself with positive material to read along with those positive people. This will help move your confidence to another level.

That process will continue to reinforce positive thinking. That way when something negative does happens you are in a much better place with better coping skills. As a result, your quality of life can move in a positive direction. It is also important that you believe in yourself. I can remember how my self-esteem, my self-confidence along with my self-image were all shattered instantly. Rebuilding them would take many tools and countless hours. Going through this process was a rather odd experience but one that would set me free in many ways. As you read on you will see that regaining them played a vital role in regaining a new identity and a new quality of life.

Anthony J Rockweiler

CHAPTER 3

THE KEY

The key I speak of here in this chapter we all have. It is a key that lies within our mind just waiting for us to unleash its potential. Meditation would help lead me to a place in my mind that was truly unknown to me. It would be a place where many of the answers would lie. Once I found that key I gained a new tool that would allow me to see my situation in a much different way.

Once I unlocked that part of my mind, my perception of the way I would see life would change forever. It would help free me from a dark place that I found myself held prisoner in for a long time. For the first time in years I could see a light piercing through giving me the hope I needed to stay alive. It was like breathing life itself back into me all over again. My perception became everything at that point. I still had many obstacles at the time that would last years after the accident, yet I can see I was beginning to look at them in a different way. I realized that many of these conditions might not go away anytime soon. Therefore, I began to accept the fact that I might have to live with some of them forever.

I had to find something to help me deal with them in a positive way. Meditating alone sent me on a journey that allowed me to save my life.

I searched for that key before and could not find it. Searching for it was like looking for something I never seen before. Still I could sense something was there. Desperation was beginning to set in. I needed something I never obtained before. I needed a miracle. Then something told me to seek the light to find the key. When I found that light which was a deep place inside my mind where my spirit would lie something would happen. I would find the key too many of the answers I needed and find a place of refuge for the first time since the accident. This place of refuge lies within each one of us.

For me, I would find true peace and serenity while there. Being in this place was a completely new experience and one that I was not familiar with at the time. All I knew then was meditation would lead me to a place where I had never been to before and open a new world for me. Once I found this place in my mind I would be able to unlock some of the mysteries that lay deep within each of us. This place would also change my view and perception of everything, including the world I once lived in. It is a place in our mind that we all have and it is a place I believe many will never use. Life changed that day for me when I tapped into that resource. I began to focus on the issues that still plagued me. Then I began to make progress in the right direction so I could gain control of my life once again.

I noticed the suffering became a little more tolerable with each passing day. My attitude began to shift and my view of life began to head in a more positive direction. It appeared as if I could hear life calling out to me for the first time in years. In the end what I would come away with, was life itself.

This doesn't mean all your problems will go away. However, I do believe your problems will no longer be the main distraction in your life. In this place you will find all the answers you need for a happy, peaceful, and fulfilling life. I believe our spirit lies deep within our mind and is always willing to help. If we listen, we can find the guidance we may need through some of the most troubled times in our life. Many times we are not patient long enough and we do not listen long enough in order for any changes to take place.

When this happened to me my world as I knew it stopped. It did not slow down. It stopped altogether. Then what I came away with that day would change the way I would see life forever. I was no longer that man I used to be in many ways. There were things in place helping me that I was not even aware of until the end. When my life came to a stop that day, I had no choice but to listen. So I asked for help and went deep within my mind. Then at some point things began to open up for me once again. The mind is such an unbelievable instrument. We do not realize how important our mind is in everyday life and what it does for us daily.

I witnessed for myself as I called on my mind for answers and it responded in a most profound way.

If you believe and I mean really believe change is possible, then change can occur. Your mind can connect to forces in a unique way that you are not even aware of, just as I did. A force that I believe was the Creator, would step in and save my life and I find that most profound. I realized there was no one coming for me. I had to believe in a way which would be much different from any belief I had before.

I have always found the human mind amazing in one way or another. When this happened to me, I found myself in dire circumstances and feeling desperate. I realized I would need to call upon resources that were not even available to me at the time. I would go searching out of desperation in order to survive and would return with a miracle, saving my life. I would gain insight and compassion along with a deeper understanding of life. I was able to accept and love myself for the man I would become. I will never forget those days. To me they are a reminder of how powerful and unique the bond between you and the Creator can be. It is a bond like no other.

I believe the human mind is one of the greatest tools at our disposal. It is incredible how we can reach inside our mind and connect to an area we never connected before and find the answers we need. What a phenomenal process to witness. I connected my mind to the force that governs the universe for healing and that is incredible.

The human mind is evolving all the time without you ever noticing it. Remember this: "None of us are who we were yesterday." It does not matter how minute or how massive something may have been yesterday it changed the way we see life forever. I also had to call upon areas of my thinking and functioning that I was not even aware of at the time. There would be certain resources built into the human mind that would step in as designed. I call them "the gifts". It was almost as if someone else stepped in to help me showing me pictures, numbers, and visions.

It was awesome and unbelievable to witness and it is still captivating today. It is amazing now as it was then—the uniqueness of the human mind seen firsthand in harmony with my belief. It was powerful. I cannot say that enough.

My instincts also began helping me in ways I was not even aware of at the time. My intuition became my best friend and grew with each passing day. I learned to trust my intuition like never before. It would be another guiding light in a desperate time and lead me out of a dark place that I was in for so long. If we believe in ourselves then the ability to change our lives becomes possible. If we believe all things are possible, it sets off a chain reaction of events like no other. No other life form on this planet has that ability. Each day be still and spend some time meditating letting your mind wind down.

Call on something greater than yourself for guidance. Your life too may change like never before just as mine did.

For me, many tools came into play as I desperately called upon them. I knew time was running out and I needed to find peace as I called on the greatest tool of all, the human mind. I knew if I were to live the answers were no longer outside of me. That is why I say to you, seek that peace within you. Call on or do something greater than yourself and your life has a way of improving. Then your problems have a way of minimizing or diminishing.

I know each one of us has that unique ability to charter to and expand our consciousness and sub-consciousness. As we grow from a child to an adult the expanding of our mind seems to subside when there is so much more we can develop. We stop calling upon it and as a result our mind stops developing in ways that could heal us and advance us. Learn to meditate even if it is just a little each day.

Allow yourself to drift into a place of silence and peace. I envisioned a place of beauty and silence where a new life awaited me. I also envisioned a place where healing myself could take place knowing that it must be an area inside of my mind I never used before. For me I continued to meditate and seek this place each day. As I did this I drifted to a deeper place of consciousness in my mind.

It was almost like being awake and asleep at the same time in the beginning. I begin to separate the chaos I was experiencing and tap into an area that would eventually save my life. I know how important being in silence truly is. In that silence you will find something you never experienced before.

Just start with perhaps fifteen minutes a day. Go to a quiet place in your home or wherever you may be, and just sit, or lie down, whichever you prefer. I close my eyes and envisioned a place of beauty, a place where I could go to where I never been before. I pictured a place where life resided and healing myself could become possible. So, you can start as I did. Close your eyes and visualize a place of beauty in your mind, it's there. A place that is still and quiet. It is a place where you will find peace and refuge from your everyday life. I envisioned a new life and a new world waiting for me. I finally found a place in my mind where these assets were waiting and a new world opened for me. So do like I did. Relax and find that calmness and peace we all seek. Just practice relaxing your mind. Imagine your hand rolled up tight in your mind and just imagine relaxing your hand. As your hand relaxes, picture your mind relaxing, bringing a calming effect. In today's society were always on the go and moving from one thing to another. We never let our mind just ease from the everyday stress so we can relax and cope.
Eventually things caught up with us manifesting in some way or another causing problems. If you push the human mind each day and never rest, then problems will arise. It is no different from any other machine, except it is the most precise in the universe. However, it has its limit. That is what I believe.

So, remember to keep repeating this process each day and in time it will become easier and feel more natural. Then it can become a part of your life just as it did for me. Find that place we all have in our mind, but never go seeking. That is where I found peace and happiness and a new life waiting for me. So I know you can too. It's also place of solace and it's there waiting for you.

For me there was something there that I could call on when all else failed and I felt desperate and alone. I believe a superior being, the Creator was there which gave me comfort and love along with a safe place of refuge. That day something extraordinary would take place as I returned with my own miracle, and a new life, realizing who holds, "The Power of Life." It is there waiting for you too. You were not born with stress and depression along with anxiety. Those conditions we impose on ourselves in one way or another over the course of our lives. They affect each one of us in a different way, especially over time. Meditating would led me to a place in my mind where I never been before which allowed me to escape the suffering. It was an instrumental and key part of my recovery. A place I went seeking for healing. It allowed me to find peace and happiness which allowed me to move forward and save my life. The relentless stress and constant pressure took a toll on me. I take some comfort in knowing that I hung in there and made it through such a difficult time in my life. Making that turn when I did meant everything.

That is why I know firsthand how things can close in on you and if you are not careful you can withdraw from life. I found myself stripped of my self-confidence, my self-esteem, and my self-image, all at once. I had a fifth-grade reading and a seventh-grade mathematics capacity after this ordeal. A man that was once confident now finds himself searching for things to help him feel complete again. You build those attributes over the course of your life. To lose them in an instant is life altering and an odd feeling. Believe me, you become lost and confused rather quickly.

Finding that belief in myself once again took me a long time under those conditions. I did not realize it at the time, but bonding with life in that way once again meant everything to me. Once that process would take place peace and happiness were right there waiting for me. I can hear them calling out, "Welcome back my friend. It has been a long time.

I can remember my ability to laugh was gone for a long time as if I had no sense of humor. I would ask the doctor about this whenever we would talk. I can remember saying on many occasions, "Where is my ability to laugh and smile?"

At one point, I had a great sense of humor and I would often find things funny. Were those moments gone and lost forever? I was a character. I loved to laugh. Yet oddly enough, those traits were not lost. They would find their way back into my life once again. That is why I believe it is important to spend some time each day alone relaxing and meditating. I know mediating opened so many doors in my life during my recovery. It gave me the tools I would need to go beyond what is normal and obtain a new normal in my life. It put me in alignment with those things I could not see. I just don't know where I would be without the ability to meditate and find that healing place which saved my life.

I can assure you the reward is tremendous and the benefits are vast. Give yourself a little time at first then you will begin to notice a difference and feel more relaxed each day. It's like many things we try to do, if you were do them just once the chances are you will not see results. I can recall when I was young I began bodybuilding around twenty five developing a good physique over the course of a couple of years. The same principle applies here in meditating. If I had meditated for just one day I would not have seen any results or changes.

However, in bodybuilding with consistency over time, I begin to notice a change in my body. Meditating is no different. The more you practice this process the better and easier it will become. It will open new doors in your life that you never knew existed. We use such a minute area of our mind. It does not take long, it just takes practice. Out of desperation, I unleashed my mind and it would lead me somewhere new and somewhere unknown. Remember, the more you meditate and go to that place in your mind the more you will feel at peace. Perhaps you will begin to see life as I did, in a new way. Then you can see for yourself "The Power of Life."

That is why it is so important to practice this technique each day. Sometimes at night when I awaken, I will relax to seek that place in my mind as I fall asleep once again. I can go to that place a little easier now than I could before. Learning these techniques and using my affirmations daily became instrumental in this process. These tools allowed me to return to a fulfilling life once again. I still tell life upon awakening how much I love it and in return it always has something interesting for me. My affirmations may seem like mere words, but they are powerful tools when reinforced each day. I believe people have an easier time relating to negative situations rather than positive. Positive affirmations can have an effect far beyond what one may believe.

Negative thinking appears to be easier to believe in. Positive thinking and positive reinforcement can open a new world for someone. It's not a process people use to any degree in this country and as a result you don't get to feel the benefits of it. You must give it some time.

I often say to people, "Tell life every day that you love it and you don't even need to believe it at first." The belief will come. Just say those words every day. Give it some time and you will find yourself waking up smiling and feeling different about life, just as I did. I know through my own experience. I said it every day for months until one day upon awakening I had a smile on my face. It was the strangest and happiest feeling.

That is when I saw once again "The Power of Life". I also felt the powerful connection each one of us can possess with this universe. I believe the Creator created life and we are that creation. We have a unique power within us through our spiritual being which can allow us to heal ourselves in many ways. For me to be able to feel the power of those experiences first hand was remarkable. I found it fascinating then and it is still an incredible feeling today.

I used mere words and repeated them over and over in my mind until I influenced my thoughts which influenced the outcome. Wow. It was an incredible feeling.

This process would take me out of a desperate situation, recreate me, and save my life. I find that so fascinating. I expanded my mind in ways I never dreamed possible. I had this feeling at a young age that the human mind was capable of incredible tasks. In this process I would learn all things are possible when you align yourself with the universe. Therefore, another aspect of my recovery and the most important one was the power of belief. I think it is the most powerful tool we have at our disposal and the most incredible.

Try to use the affirmations I speak of here in my story to see if they can influence your own circumstances. Over the course of time it is possible something can change in you as you recite them. Your belief will deepen and your connection with this universe can begin to alter. It is possible that you will see life in a different perspective than before. It is possible that you will begin to see yourself and the people around you in a different way than before. I think you just may view the world as a remarkable and rather fascinating place. Why not try it, you have nothing to lose and everything to gain. A richer and fuller life is there waiting for you just as it was for me.

In my case I went seeking the power of the universe through belief and that power stepped in saving my life. If I would have continued down the road I was on I might not be alive today. I am so thankful things went the way they did.

Anthony J Rockweiler

Chapter 4

THE PLACE

I mention this in the previous chapter, "The Place". Throughout my life I went to a place in my mind believing that I could achieve or learn something new by going into my mind to find the answers. Even as a young boy I knew we must have the ability to heal ourselves. I just didn't know how. To escape the chaos I was in from this ordeal I began going within my mind to create or find a healing place I knew existed. I practiced meditation each day and I would allow my mind to drift into this place, seeking peace. My hope was to escape the suffering I found myself in for so long. It became a place in my mind where everything was still and quiet. I would find the safety I needed at a desperate time. One of the first times I can recall going to this place was years before this ordeal. I can recall going there when I started bodybuilding in my twenties. This was eleven years before the accident would take place.

I remember I could drift into this place or state of

mind while I was exercising. It would allow me to isolate myself from the outside world.

It was like being in my own world or my own place and nothing else mattered at the time. It was a way I could exercise making progress and development with my physique while I was in a peaceful place at the same time. It was just me and life.

When this situation came into play I would need to seek this "Place" at a deeper level if I was going to survive. It was difficult dealing with so many medical conditions at the same time and trying to find this new place. My circumstances were relentless day after day. The psychological suffering from the noise alone would push anyone to the edge at any moment. It was always dangerously scary. Dealing with this alone would push me to a place in my mind I never knew existed. Each of these experiences pushed me to a new area in my mind in order to survive. Think about this, you cannot turn it off and there is no escaping it. I felt like I must find a place of peace where I could survive before time ran out or I may not make it. I was the type of person who could handle stress well before this happened. Yet, this was a much different type of stress. There were many occasions when I wondered how much more I could tolerate or how close I was to the edge. One doctor stated to me, "Everyone has a breaking point," and I wondered how close I was many times to that breaking point. That is why it was so important that I found this place in my mind once again and find it as soon as possible.

This time I would need to go much deeper into my mind for a longer period to find what I called a new "place". In this new place, I would find refuge once again. It was not easy, especially at first. It would take much longer and a great deal of patience as I went deeper than before to discover a new "place."

Meditating daily in the midst of all the chaos proved to be quite challenging. There were many conflicting obstacles taking place in my mind all at once.

The physical conditions I suffered from only compounded the situation even more. Therefore, when I did find the new "place" in my mind, it would look much different than before. Finding myself in this situation allowed me to see that I could go within my mind to heal myself. I know finding that place under those conditions would turn out to be another test of survival. At first I didn't know if it would be possible to find it, or if I did, what would be the outcome. I know something drove me each day to try and I kept saying to myself, "It must be close. It must be close. Hang on." Therefore, I hung on until I finally broke through.

That place exists in each one of us. It is a place in our mind where we can find peace, the kind of peace we all seek. For me, once I reached this place I would find that peace and return with a much different view of life. It was not like anything I experienced before.

I believe if you apply the principles I speak of, it is possible you too can see a change in your quality of life.

My friends on occasions have asked me at times if I would go speak to one of their friends or loved ones that was going through something at the time. They found themselves in a similar situation and trapped emotionally for whatever reason. Something took place in their own life that was keeping them from moving forward.

I found myself reaching out to these individuals and showing them a great life is not far away. It is closer than you think. Our circumstances may be different, but our outcome can be the same. You can return to a better quality of life.

I wanted them to hear my story and let them know that whatever they are dealing with they can still improve. Many may think they cannot gain a better quality of life, but I believe they can. I believe people can reach a better quality of life just by reaching out. Perhaps they may have thought they reached their true potential, but I find many times that is not the case. Many people may not realize this, but their true potential is way out there in front of them. Sometimes I think their support system may not be creating the environment for improvement. The people I speak with I share my perspective mentioning not to let society dictate your recovery and improvement.

I have heard at times that their friends or relatives were telling them to accept where they were. You are not going to get any better. To accept the situation for what it is. To me there is nothing wrong with accepting where you are, but there can be room for improvement.

I would explain the process of positive reinforcement to whoever it may be. I would also explain some of my principles to them about moving forward and gaining a better quality of life. I would try to express how important it is to view life in a positive way. See life as your friend just as I do. I know it can be hard at times. Some things may seem like you cannot overcome them. Allow the process to unfold and you can see that you can move forward to a fulfilling life. You can reach a new level just as I did. If I would have accepted that mentality of what other people said, I may not be alive today. Throughout my life I never let people or society in general dictate what I could or could not do. Only I knew my true potential and as a result I overcame many challenges and I know you can too. Believe that you can overcome and achieve and you will.

I speak with people all the time and many of them find it difficult to find that belief they will need to overcome. Some people have said to me, "If I only had someone like you around me for motivation." This saddens me when I hear this because I realize there may be no one in his or her life that can help or make a difference. I know it can be difficult, but do not give up on yourself because you are your greatest asset.

You can improve your situation and remember life is your friend. For me, I accept where I am at that particular time, but I know I can improve. There is always room for improvement and I am always pushing forward each day to make some progress. Life should be fun and not a constant battle to survive. I accept what life gives me each day and make peace and happiness my number one goal.

I challenged myself in this process to improve every

day, even if it was just a little. Going to that place of safe haven in my mind each day became important to me. My situation changed because I found that place of peace in my mind that would alter everything. That played a huge role in saving my life and bringing happiness and enjoyment back to me as well. I was able to escape my circumstances when all else failed and that became so important for my survival. It gave me a safe refuge each time I went to "the place". I believe a greater presence was always there with me, comforting me, even when I was not aware of it. I would end up going there more and more with each passing day seeking a deeper peace and comfort. I know for the first two years I slept as much as possible to cope and escape.

It was around this period of time I began seeking that place in my mind each day. When I was finally able to get there I would find the tools necessary in order to save my life and be happy once again. Peace and serenity would also be there waiting for me in my new world. Coping became a little easier as each day passed and I began to improve. Although it took me some time I tried my best to remain positive each day. I found myself in an odd place without traits I once possessed such as self-confidence and self-esteem. Therefore, it would take me some time to regain them and find my way back.

As I began to see hope creep back into my life, I could see my circumstances beginning to improve. Of course it was not fast enough for me, but it gave me the strength I needed at that time to hold on. I was able to make that agreement with life once again. I could feel the bond that only life and I could share. I wanted to live in peace and happiness and have that passion for living once again. It took me some time because I had so many issues to deal with.

I am proud of the fact that I hung in there throughout this process and did not give up on myself. Even when my situation appeared hopeless I continued to push forward. I cannot lie to you it was difficult and I found myself desperate at times. The circumstances were frightening and overwhelmed me for a long time. I did manage to hang on to hope by a thread and make that critical turn.

I consider myself lucky. I can remember standing on the edge several times throughout this process not knowing if I would truly make it. Giving up would have been the easy thing to do. Yet the easiest thing to do is not always the best thing to do. Life laid that out for me firsthand. Your life experiences become your greatest teacher.

I knew somehow as a young boy that healing through our mind would one day be possible. Years later I would need to put that notion to the test. I influenced my thoughts over and over which would eventually lead me out of a dark place to recover my life. Never give up hope. Believe change is possible and change will come. A new world can open for you just as it did for me. Be open and visualize the life you want. This will allow you to create the world you want to live in, by perception. Old memories and difficult situations will begin to diminish drifting farther from your day-to-day life. Make time for yourself each day by relaxing and meditating. This can release the stress from your everyday life. Remember you must believe change is possible and your life can change bringing you a better quality of life, just as it did for me.

Remember the best things in life do not come easy. When I look back on this ordeal I realize this process has been like a test. I find myself recreated because of this journey into the person I am today. I came away with a great deal of knowledge and wisdom about life and myself. I am grateful to be alive. I took the tools and lessons life provided me back into a new world along with a new perception of life.

Chapter 5

Act As If

These three words alone still send chills down my spine. I can recall these words in the early stages of this process calling out to me like a long lost friend. These words, "act as if" would prove to be so powerful and compelling in my recovery. I had no idea the impact or role they would play especially at the time. I continue to use these words every day and every day they reveal and produce something new to me. These words can alter your world and everything in it much quicker than you think. All you need to do is allow them to take effect. These words, "act as if", are also based on belief and thought reinforcement. If you just say the words your thoughts will become your reality. This process brought me a better quality of life. What does it mean when you hear the words "act as if"? I am going to show you what they did for me and how they can work for you too.

"Acting as if" you already have the life you want will begin to set off a chain reaction of events meant only for you.

You will begin to see life itself and the world around you in a different way. This is not about material possessions. It is about bringing yourself in harmony with life itself. Then everything in your life takes on a different meaning, whether it is material or not. Your view and appreciation for anything materialistic will change as well. Material things such as cars and houses are nice, but I do not need them. What I want and what I need are two different things. What I need to have is peace, happiness, and be in harmony with life. As long as I have that everything else will be just fine. I realized I own nothing. Everything was here when I came and it will be here when I am gone. Life takes on a new meaning when you begin to realize that.

Those three words are powerful and I am living proof of that. I remember trying to juggle so many obstacles at one time. I can recall how these words would help me recover my life. Every day was a chaotic situation. Once things set in on me, I was a mess. After that I was not sure about anything. The man that went to work that day vanished. I became another person instantly. I was bright and articulate one minute and then confused and lethargic the next. I went to work one man and came home another asking myself many days, "Who am I?" Of course none of us are who we were yesterday.

Yet this was an instant change by normal means. I had many questions and there was so much uncertainty surrounding the situation. If I was going to survive this ordeal at all I knew my belief and faith would be the answer. This was a much different situation altogether and one that I never experienced before. What happened that day in May altered the course of my life and my family's lives forever. When something like this passes through your life it affects everyone around. You begin to see the world in a different way than you did before. There was a great deal of uncertainty about my family and our future. I didn't understand many things at the time or the impact of what exactly was taking place. So when those three simple words came into play they would prove to be another turning point in my recovery.

They would play a role in sculpting me into the man I am today. They were vital in this process. Without them I don't know where I would be today. Throughout this process words begin to take on a new and different meaning to me, especially these words. I still use these simple words every day. I had to start acting like I was happy and smiling when I was not happy at all. I had to start acting confident when I was not confident at all. I began to act out the emotions I wanted way before I had them. I started acting like the person I wanted to be and creating that person in the process. That was profound and difficult early on. When someone asked me how I was doing I had to answer, "I'm doing fine. Thank you," when I was not doing well at all. I was still dealing with quite a few conditions at the time that made it difficult to function. So telling people I was doing well when in fact I was not would prove to be another test.

I had to start saying and "acting as if" I was smart and confident when I was not smart and confident at all. I had to "act as if" nothing was bothering me when everything was. I found this challenging and difficult to do every day especially when knew I was no longer confident and smart. Yet, combining these three words along with my affirmations became second nature to me. As a result, one day I actually found myself smiling without forcing myself to do so. I actually woke up one morning with a smile on my face. It was then I began to see the power in the words I was using.

I remember asking my doctor one day, "How come I do not laugh anymore like I used to? I was a funny person and had a great sense of humor. Is something wrong with me now? Where is my ability to laugh? Is it gone?" I know I had a lot to deal with at the time, but it just seemed like something was not right. Something was wrong and I could not put my finger on it. I appeared to be doing this self-analysis on myself from time to time. My physician would speak of the different medical conditions I was dealing with as the cause. It just seemed like something else was wrong. Therefore, when I did catch myself smiling one day it was such a good and powerful feeling. It felt so gratifying especially under those conditions. Even though the smile did not last long it reinforced the power of those words and my belief system. You can change brain chemistry by thought. The only problem was the feeling did not stay with me very long, perhaps only a few minutes each day. I can remember the sensation it gave me. It was such a sense of empowerment, especially at that time. It made me feel as though I was beginning to recover my life at such a desperate time. I wanted it to stay with me but it would slowly slip away.

I kept saying, "I want to be happy, and at peace, and love life all over again, like I used to. I want to have that passion for living, like before." I kept saying, "Act as if everything is okay," over and over again. I kept saying, "I want to be at peace and happiness with life more than ever." It was hard early on, but I continued doing it every day until I started to see some results. I had to believe and believe like never before. I had nothing else but my belief.

I can remember when I first began to see a change. It was like a glimmer of light giving me the hope I needed to hang on. I trusted my instincts more than ever as they began to assist me more and more. My instincts would be another valuable tool. Those victories may have been small but they gave me hope that I could find my way out and return to a fulfilling life. I kept at it each day and pushed forward. I knew it was crucial that I find that place once again and using these words would only help.

I knew my survival depended on it. I knew this much.

I did not want to continue going down the road I was on. I felt like time was running out and I needed to make a turn and make it soon.

Every day I would say, "I am smart. I am keen. I am bright," until these things finally started to set in. I believe one of the gifts in our creation is the ability to heal ourselves through our mind. Alone you can do only so many things, yet when connected to a higher power a completely new world opens up. Then you step into another dimension. A dimension where all things become possible as a much greater force steps in.

This journey would test me in so many ways. The biggest, "act as if" moment for me was when I had to act like the man I used to be before the accident. That was powerful and a life-altering situation. Seeing him and not being him was like being happy and sad at the same time. Therefore, each day I would try to act like him and mimic his ways such as his personality and old traits instilling them into me once again. It took me plenty of time and patience's. In the end when things settled down a new man would emerge. A higher power would step in and recreate me.

I found that love all over again for the person I would become. When I look back now I can say that I stayed relentless and my belief remained strong. It was a lesson I will always remember.

Oh yes, I was afraid many days. It seemed like most of the time I drifted along searching for myself wondering, "Who am" I or "who will I be". I remember shedding many tears on those days and nights wondering if I would find my way or if I would ever make that turn. There were days when I wanted to give up, but I would find another key and remain hopeful. It appeared as if, each time I felt like time was running out I would find a new tool that gave me the hope to move forward. Those were desperate days. At times it was difficult because I wanted to get better, but it seemed like it was taking forever. I wanted to improve, but life reminded me of patience every single day. That is another lesson I take away from this ordeal. I will always take what life gives me and be as patient as I can. By doing so I will have everything I need—maybe not everything I want, but surely everything I need.

Remember, life is always in control. I now find myself more in harmony with life than before. I also feel that I am more comfortable with who I am now than before. I find that odd considering I would need to transform from one person to another. I would come to understand and love myself all over again. This process provided many tools and re-created me into the person I am now. The injuries I dealt with made it difficult to speak and I found myself not going out because of fear. I could not carry on conversations or articulate sentences well at all. Gathering the correct words took a tremendous amount of effort. Yet, as time would have it, all those things would change. Although it would take me some time and patience words continued to open a new world and a new life for me.

Today I meet and speak with many people on a daily basis and it seems so easy. By speaking with me you would never know what happened and that became another powerful characteristic of this unbelievable journey. This journey has been incredible and has altered the way I view life itself. It has changed me in countless ways and in the process it freed me. This so called misfortune opened what were once boundaries to me and expanded my mind to new horizons. Thus, revealing to me a completely new area of life that I will never forget. For those things I am grateful. Every day I "act as if" and use another precious tool to advance my life and you can too if you just give it a chance to work.

Believe in yourself, love yourself, and take care of yourself. Then your world too can change right before your eyes. There is no need for me to "act as if" I love life anymore. I found that love for myself once again and you can too. If you find yourself struggling just try these words: "act as if, and see what happens. These simple words can help bring a new world to you and can bring you out of a desperate situation just as they did for me. I found a new identity for myself in the process. These three words played a pivotal role in my recovery and allowed me to find happiness once again.

Those words would prove to be another turning point in my life. When I am out in the everyday world people approach me at times. Many ask me about my physique and my age. Some just appear to call me over to them and say there's something different about you. I just laugh, because I know want it is. They may ask me how they can lose weight and get a better quality of life.

I always point out how your diet alone can sculpture your body. I also point out to them the tools I acquired in my recovery process. I always mention my "act as if" concept and the way I used it to bring me a better life. I may ask them about their perception of life itself. I also ask how they perceive their own life. I believe there is a correlation between the two that can determine the quality of life you will live. You should perceive life as your friend and embrace it each day for the gift that it is. Wake up each morning and tell life how much you love it and continue to do that until you actually believe it.

I also mention this concept: if you were to exercise for one day you will not see any results. Just like if you were to diet for one day you would see no results either. It is consistency over time that helps determine the progress and results. The same concept stands true for the "act as if" principle and the way you perceive life. If you do these techniques over time than you too may yield the same results I did. Even the way you see this world may begin to change as a better life comes your way.

Then you may find the energy to do the things you like to do along with the energy and desire to take care of yourself in a completely different way. I know those things were hard for me to do when I found myself in the midst of this ordeal especially early on.

However, one of the most important aspects will be that you believe in yourself. Many people seem to be concerned with the way they look or their weight and they should be. Your health is important. Yet, if you have a passion for living and envision life as a true gift you may begin to see happiness in a different way.

For example, you may see it in a beautiful sunrise or in the mystic of a beautiful night as darkness falls. You may begin to see happiness in everything you do and everything you say. You may also begin to feel a sense of peace and comfort like you never experienced before.

When you become more in harmony with life, and just waking up and being happy, you begin to live as one with life. A sense of peace will come over you and even the people around you will begin to notice it. For me, because of my new perception of life a sense of empowerment came along that I did not possess before. People seem to approach me now when I am out in the everyday world differently than they did before. At times, they say, "There is something about you. You are different." To me when you flow in harmony with life there is an energy or aura that people can see coming from you. It seems to make them curious in some way or another. I even had people come up to me and say, "You seem so happy, and friendly." At first it seemed odd and I wondered where these people were coming from and what did they see in me.

I noticed it did not matter where I was or what I was doing. That appeared to be another odd aspect of this process as time went on. The feeling seemed to get stronger and stronger over time as it appeared to take on its own meaning. It was a feeling I never experienced before. It would once again reinforce the "Power of Life". Over the course of time I just got accustomed to it. I am not sure what it was except the fact that I see my life and this world in a different way than before. I know each one of us can have this capability.

I learned so much about how you can influence

your thoughts and in return you can influence the outcome. For example, I influenced my thoughts through words in a positive way. In return I recaptured my personality traits along with my self-confidence. I noticed by thinking this way it seems to bring positive change into my everyday life. It can be just the opposite when we think negative thoughts. I think people can understand negative thoughts can create a negative outcome.

For example, if someone remains negative over time, then the possibility of falling into depression increases. I am not sure if people understand that you can influence that process in a positive way and come away with positive results. Think about it, I used mere words and thoughts, and influenced my way out of a dark place and back to a better life.

Anyone can apply these words just as I did. I used them daily and recovered my life. First, just begin by saying the words, "act as if" and reinforce them daily and watch what happens. You must believe it is possible and change will come. Then just give it some time. So, whatever obstacle you may be trying to overcome or if there is something you are seeking in your life, "act as if" you have it already or try to envision whatever may be coming to you, just as I did. I could see the changes manifest as I used these words daily. I would begin to act smart and confident when I did not feel smart and confident at all. I began envisioning my vocabulary expanding before it expanded. I began smiling when I didn't feel like smiling. These simple words would become another vital tool in my recovery.

For me I continued to "act as if" I had what I wanted and I believed the results would come. Therefore, I know it is possible that someone can achieve the same results that I did. Then you too will have the ability to perceive life and the world you live in in a different way, just as I did. I used these simple words which help bring me back to a new world where a fulfilling life was waiting.

The human mind has a remarkable ability to perform day-to-day task that we are not even aware as we go about our day. There are certain areas that we can call upon to assist us in the healing process. I believe we are not educated on how to access our mind in a useful way that could help us further advance our life. I always knew the mind had these incredible abilities even at a young age. It was not until I found myself in this situation that I had to call upon resources in my mind that I never knew existed. I know these assets are just lying there in our mind, dormant and waiting for us to call upon them. I would call upon these gifts and depend upon my mind in a way I never did before as it led me to a new world and a new life.

Chapter 6

Serenity

Serenity, it was there waiting on me. Remember, in the midst of chaos lies serenity. Even as a young boy I found amazement and wonder about this world, and this universe, along with life itself.

There were many days where I would sit and wonder about so many things. Where did I come from, who am I, and where do we go from here. I knew there was a much larger picture than what appeared in my everyday life. Man says the universe exploded when it was created. Then where did the explosion come from? What space and time was involved to bring this into perspective. Science cannot explain it. Who or what brought the creation of everything into play. It was just a lot of questions I found myself asking and not knowing who or where to go to at a young age to find the answers. I do not think especially back then, there were many kids wondering about such things. The ability to heal ourselves, where did we come from, who am I, and where am I going to from here.

Throughout my life these thoughts always seemed to influence my thinking on a much larger scale about this world and how we got here.

When I was around eight years old, I would take watches and clocks apart and fix them. At twelve, it was motorcycles. When I was fourteen I bought my first automobile for 35 dollars and I disassembled it. Then, I built my own automobile and drove it to high school at fifteen. At sixteen and seventeen I built my own high-performance car. I was always looking for some way to advance myself. Searching and looking for a task a little bit more difficult in order to challenge myself as I was growing up. I always appeared to have this belief in myself even when I was young. Even then the human mind amazed me in some way or another. I found it fascinating. I realized the potential of the human mind early on in my life as I stated before. I always had this feeling when I was a young boy that the human mind was creative and had abilities beyond our understanding. Even then, I felt the brain held creativity and potential we would never understand. I believe a higher power put everything into play and created our mind with certain abilities. In addition, through meditation we would have the ability to bring a better quality of life to ourselves and have the ability to heal ourselves in the process. For the same reason, we can focus on positive thoughts and bring positive change into our life. Also, by doing this I believe you can influence the ability to bring positive people into your life.

I can remember building cars and creating things when I was a young boy, tapping into certain resources that were truly amazing. I would always stand back afterwards and look at what I created. I always felt a sense of peace and empowerment seeing the results.

Being young I would let my mind wonder each day as I approached another project learning something new and creating a deeper sense of accomplishment.

You know I can see as I grew from a young boy into a man how disassembling things and re-assembling them would give me an understanding of a priceless lesson. So many people over the course of my life have asked me, who showed you how to fix watches and build cars at such a young age along with bodybuilding, I said no one. They would reply do you understand that is not normal. I would say, well, I never thought about it. I do know over the course of my life and even when I was young I never let anyone tell me what my abilities were or were not. I never let society tell me I could not do something because of my age or my ability or my education. Only I knew my potential, no one else did.

Once again I see the parallels between what I did when I was young and what I did throughout this ordeal. I took those tools I developed throughout my life and used them to reconstruct and rebuild a new life for myself once again. I would also build a unique bond with life that would be stronger than before. Don't ever think the things you are doing today will not be useful tomorrow.

You never know when you may need to call upon what you learned yesterday in order to save your life today. Those resources are invaluable.

Remember, no one needs to come and show you necessary, how to do something. Believe in yourself. There are so many tools today at your fingertips. Computers, books, and with the internet you can gain access to so much more. Let your mind wonder and a completely new world can open for you just as it did for me.

People have a way of walking into your life when you think that way. They seem to come out of nowhere. Those very people supply you with an even more resourceful tool and that is another human mind.

I can see by having this mindset of disassembling objects when I was young and building new ones better than before would play a vital role in my recovery. When I was young I would take parts from many automobiles and make one nice, fast car. That process became more natural to me as I applied it over time. It made me more and more resourceful especially at a young age. I was doing things at a young age that young people had no concept of doing at the time. I applied that principle throughout my young life and it brought me more resources than I could never imagine, especially at a critical time. I believed engaging with my mind in order to heal myself was possible at a young age. Also at a young age I believed there must be something much greater than myself that created everything making us unique in the process.

Later I realized this type of thinking laid the groundwork for what I would need in order to survive.

I believe it was a preparation for what was to come at the age of thirty-six. I found myself using those same principles which allowed me to piece myself back together. I used some of my old personality along with building a new personality with the tools life provided.

It is ironic when I think about it, when I was young I took pieces of many cars to make one automobile, sleeker, faster and better than new. Later in life after the injury I implemented some of those same principles and ideas, applying different pieces of myself, some old, and some new, and came out with the man I am today.

I went to work one man on that beautiful Monday morning and would come home another. So you see here once again I would need to rebuild myself similar to bodybuilding, but only this time in a much more intricate and difficult way. This would be the ultimate challenge where resources from the past would surface, and automatically step in to help me rebuild and recover my life. It was as if someone else stepped in to help me. I am so lucky I had those tools because they were priceless and became so valuable. I utilized what I taught myself at a young age, being resourceful. That type of thinking would emerge from my youth to help save my life. I believe we have so many tools within our mind and at our fingertips. Your mind is so valuable. Never forget that. You can be the best tool you have.

Your mine is your greatest asset. Do not wait for a

miracle because you can be one by believing in yourself or helping someone else. There are many ways to create a miracle. A smile on a desperate day for someone can be a miracle. You just never know what someone is going through from day to day. A sense that someone cares can be a miracle. The wonder of life is a miracle itself. Encouraging others can be, or lead to a miracle. I learned by doing these things it could bring you a sense of peace that you may not otherwise have or had.

Using positive words and reinforcing positive thoughts can bring a better life to you or someone else. You can also bring a sense of well-being and calmness into your life by this process alone.

I always had this feeling when I was young that the human mind had the ability to do remarkable things. Yet, little did I know that down the road I would need to use my mind in an unbelievable way in order to save my life.

In some regards, I believe life was preparing me for this ordeal long before the age of thirty-six. At a young age my mind was revealing to me what was to come although I had no idea at the time. I would find out for myself if these things would be possible as my life would unfold and those resources would surface.

For me, peace and happiness would be my ultimate test which would eventually set me free.

This process would also teach me about the power we can all generate from within us. You must be willing to believe it is possible in order for healing to take place. My belief would need to be much stronger than before this happen if I was going to survive.

Then, in time, through meditation a power I could not explain would step in and alter my life. I am thankful every day that I made that turn when I did. Many things became clear to me through this healing process. I call them the gifts which were the knowledge and resources given to me that allowed me to move forward and recover a new life.

Try to reinforce daily the principles I speak of here in my passages. Concentrate, meditate, and believe change is possible and change can transpire.

I know it is possible to move forward through difficult times in your life and find happiness. Many times happiness is much closer than you think. Upon waking each day now, I still stand in amazement with life. The scale on which I measure happiness and sadness has changed. Now when I see the sunrise on a beautiful day it still mystifies me. I thank the power that governs this great universe that I am alive.

My perception of many things changed in an instant as my life began to come back to me once again. I believe I am still that funny person who loves life more with each passing day.

I found that little boy in me once again and I hope I never lose him.

I see happiness in a much different way than before. For me it is much easier to achieve. I was happy with life before this process, but now my perception of life and my love for it has deepened. I went through a rough period in my life, but my passion for living has returned to me. For quite some time the situation was unreal and chaotic.

At the time, I didn't know if it would ever be possible to come back and live a productive life again. I dealt with so many obstacles and roadblocks at one time and major ones at that. It took me awhile to find that place of peace and happiness again. We all seek that serene place. I found it and you can too. I admit I had to rely on myself in ways I never did before. I had to draw from resources that were new and trust myself at a time when I thought I could not. I was afraid many days and many nights. I made some decisions out of desperation and I would trust in myself in ways I never dreamed possible. If you try some of the tools that I lay out here in my story your path to happiness could be much quicker than mine.

Whenever something happened to me in my life, I moved up to a new level of awareness. As a result, each time I would learn a great deal about myself, and the world I lived in. The process of life seems to evolve that way. When something happens to us in life we must try our best to accept it and move forward.

Many times the only way we grow is by gaining new life experiences, therefore gaining new knowledge.

Whatever ordeal or situation you may have been through in your life you found a way to deal with it and grow as a result. That process allows you to move forward as you learn from each new experience.

However, there can be times when you find it difficult to move forward. As a result, you can open the door for allowing problems or conditions to set in. These conditions can begin to compound if you are not careful. You must try to put whatever it may be in a manageable perspective as soon as possible. If not, you will get stuck in one place and limit your progress. Things can begin to set in at that point and a cycle of negative thinking can occur. If you are not careful a downward pattern can start and your quality of life can begin to diminish.

I read about people who have lived to be one hundred years of age or older. They called them

"Centenarians." There was a study performed on them to see what they all had in common or shared which allowed them to reach that age. Besides the fact that they all took care of themselves, there seem to be one characteristic that stood out. On average, each one of them seemed to have the ability to recover from grief different from the people around them. They would take in what happened, grieve over it, and put it into manageable perspective.

As a result this allowed them to move forward in a healthy way. This would reduce a great deal of stress throughout their life. I believe healthier and happy people live longer than others do.

I recall when I began exercising at twenty-five. The people who impressed me the most were older than me. They were in their thirties, forties and fifties, and so on.

I knew they had setbacks of their own to deal with over the course of their lives. They would need to overcome these setbacks in order to return to a great quality of life. What impressed me was their tenacity and passion for living, coupled with their mindset.

These characteristics would allow them to return to a positive place in their life. They would find peace and serenity within themselves. This process would lead them back to happiness rather quickly once again.

I believe the same principle is at work here. Seek happiness each day and your mind will create that feeling of peace by creating that reality. Wake up and find happiness with just being alive. Find a passion for loving and living life and then all the things you do you will be passionate about. Then peace will find its way into your life rather than you searching for peace each day. For me the healing process began to move forward in a healthy way because of this form of thinking. When I was able to sort through my emotions and put them into some type of perspective, I also began to see my life improve.

My perception of many things, especially life, would change rather quickly. I feel fortunate and thankful that I had a belief before this happened. It would lead me to my destiny where a greater power would save my life. I came away with a miracle by believing it was possible. In an instant my thinking and perception on many things begin to change that day. Because of that process I realized the world I came back to was no longer the world I remembered. Your life experiences have a way of creating the reality you live in. If you reach out to life it has a way of taking care of you.

My belief would lead me into a peaceful place in my mind where easing my emotions would be critical. That day something transpired that I still cannot explain by normal reasoning. As a result I began to see my circumstances in a different way. I realized how I drifted into my mind to find a place where a greater presence than I could ever imagine would alter my life and me, forever. I would also find serenity and a safe place of refuge there waiting for me. As my perception of life began to change I started to seek enjoyment once again. As I look back now I realize life called upon me in ways I still find fascinating as I believed my way to a miracle. Always remember you can play a role in pulling yourself out of what seems like a hopeless situation. Believe something can and will change and it can become possible.

Believe a greater power can always alter your life and miracles can become a reality. You can find your way just as I did and live a happy and productive life once again. You can also return to the things you once enjoyed. I think you too would find it amazing and perhaps unbelievable if you could have seen where I came from. When I read my own story I still find it remarkable that I am here and made it back. It seems too unreal for any human being to return from such an ordeal.

It is for that very reason I say this: you should never give up hope, even if it seems like you are hanging on by a thread. Sometimes we may not realize how close we are to making that turn before things brighten up. Happiness can be right around the corner. Many times it is closer than you think. Serenity and love are always there waiting for you.

Peace and happiness are located within you.

It is not something external you go out searching for

it is something inside of you. They are within your mind and created by how you perceive them. Finding peace and loving yourself is another important key to living the best quality of life you can. For me, finding peace and serenity when I did was crucial to my survival.

I remember when desperation was beginning to set in and I needed to make that turn and make it as soon as possible. It became clear to me that time was running out. I was fortunate to be able to find the key that would lead me to peace and happiness. It would ease my suffering and allow me to move forward. Looking back on the situation I can see how I connected with life on a different level. There is an energy that surrounds me now or a heightened sense of awareness that I did not possess before. I seem to flow with life much easier than before; as if that is the way it was meant to be. Serenity seems to be a good word for it. One could also call it peace and calmness. That is why I say in the midst of chaos lies serenity. It is like a hurricane. There is total chaos, but in the eye of a hurricane you will find blue skies and calmness. In the center of this storm I connected to a greater power and recovered my life. The peace, calmness, and happiness were already there in my mind just waiting. All I had to do was find the key which was not an easy task at first, especially when there was so much going on within me. When I did I was able unlocked the door that held me prisoner for so long. Meditation would lead me to a place where my life would never be the same. That day altered who I was forever as I believe a greater power stepped in. I walked out from sadness and sorrow and into the light once again and returned with a miracle. I thank God for allowing me to find my way to the place where all things would become possible.

Once there, my situation improved each day and became brighter as time went on. I dealt with and accepted my circumstances by viewing them in a different way. I kept reinforcing my affirmations daily as my perception of life would never be the same. My thoughts begin to shift and happiness would find its way back into my life and be my friend once again. I felt as if my life was coming together and this process was molding me into a new person all over again.

Always remember, that the power of belief can be a powerful force in your life. It is possible that your belief can return your life back to you once again, by believing so. I still use my positive affirmations daily. Every day I still witness positive people coming into my life. This is important too, do not forget to find and read inspiring stories. They will only help elevate your life to a new level. Someone once mention this to me: if you would like to see where you are going to be in five years, look around you. Look at the people you associate with and look at your environment. I guess it is somewhat like looking into the future. If those situations are negative, I do not consider that environment to someone's advantage. Create the world you want to live in by thinking positive and saying positive affirmations to yourself and then watch how your environment altars. That is what I did. I had nothing and created a new place with a new life and returned to a new world. Negativity breeds negativity until you find yourself engulfed with despair.

I just cannot see how someone can thrive and find peace in situations that appear to be negative day after day. Never let anyone tear your character down. That is the only thing you have. Remember, possessions and material objects will come and go, but not your character. I believe if you put out negative energy into this world than you will draw in negative energy. Think good things will happen to you and they will.

The universe has a way of bringing positive people into your life and making it so much better. As you begin to see new people come into your life you may not realize where they are coming from. As your perception changes you may realize that some of these very people were there all along. It is important to build a relationship with yourself by loving and caring for yourself. I wake up every day and I tell life how much I love it. I love the man I became through this process. There is always hope. Never give up on yourself. I know you will be happy with the results of loving yourself alone. Imagine if the great minds of the world would have given up on a project when it appeared hopeless. Right when they were on the verge of creating something that would change the world forever. Then the advances in science and technology you see today would not have been possible. As a result our lives would be more difficult today. We would not have the advancements in medicine or cures for diseases that we have today. It is important for you to push forward every day just as they did. I know it can be hard at times. Life can feel like it is closing in on you, but finding a better quality of life is possible. It appeared as if there was no returning from where I came from and here I am. The impossible became possible. Believing in yourself alone has an outreach much farther than you can imagine.

You can change circumstances in your life by thought alone. Also put your belief in a greater power, a power much greater than you can imagine and watch how your life changes. Many times I believe people are closer to happiness than they may realize. They may give up for whatever reason and accept things for the way they are. Sometimes they may not realize just how close they are to finding true peace and happiness. I have seen people in difficult situations who never return to productive lives. They appear satisfied with the function they may have at the time and that is fine. I think some people may give up for whatever reason not realizing a better quality of life could be close by. If you would just push a little harder the improvement will come. I have seen some people undergo surgery for example and suffer difficulties afterwards. Some may have a difficult time returning to a productive life. Some people have certain individuals around them telling them to accept things for the way they are. "You're not going to improve," they say. Some may do it out of control or some may not believe their friend or loved one can make any more progress. I think finding a better quality of life may be difficult when this atmosphere surrounds you. I have seen people who have gone through eleven years of school only to quit in the twelfth grade. I know many of those people go on to be happy and live successful lives regardless. Yet, for some I believe it is about finishing something you started.

When you finish that race there is a sense of accomplishment that comes over you. Afterwards, it gives you a sense of peace and accomplishment that you can carry forever. That is true in whatever you do.

Yet there may be times when you may not realize how close you are to finishing something before you give up. That may be the most important thing of all. You are the biggest investment you have. Without investing in yourself you cannot give anything to anyone else. I believe we must find happiness and peace within ourselves if we are to experience the true meaning of life. One should perpetuate the other bringing a sense of peace until we master the feeling. Then when something negative happens to you, you are in a better place to deal with whatever it may be. When I am out in the everyday world I meet people and I listen to their particular situation. I can see they're going through something and struggling themselves. As we speak I try to share whatever it may be that can bring them a better quality of life.

As we continue to speak I share my story with them. I mention how I was once in a hopeless situation myself just barely clinging to life. Never give up hope. It is the bridge between your circumstances and a better life. As I share my story with them they find it amazing when I tell them the things I had to overcome in order to survive. Seeing me and hearing the story does not seem to correlate or make any sense. They say it looks like there is nothing wrong with you. I just mention that a great deal went into my recovery to bring together the outcome they see now. I had a great deal of rehab and good physicians. I even live with some of residual effects from the accident, but you would never know it by looking at me. Never give up hope and never count yourself out of what may appear to be a desperate and hopeless situation. I came back from a tragedy that many may not believe was possible and regained my life once again and you can too.

You see surviving would have been one thing. On the other hand, I believe finding peace and regaining your life once again is another story. When people see me I appear fine and they can see that I am in a peaceful place. I found myself at a point in this process where I was able to put things in a manageable perspective. This allowed me to move forward with happiness. I made that agreement with life. I made the choice to live life with a passion once again. You cannot see it any other way and it would not do you any good if you did. If you dwell on the past you will not be able to move forward and find the quality of life you are looking for.

My belief made all the difference in the world. It gave me hope to hang on. Then a force much greater than I could imagine would alter my perception of life and me forever. Happiness is not about the situation you may find yourself in it is about how you respond to that situation you find yourself in. Happiness is all around you. All you need to do is just reach out for it and a better life will come.

That is why I say, when you wake up tomorrow, you might as well wake up and be happy. Peace and happiness was easier to achieve when we were kids. Yet somewhere along the line we allowed stress and the pressure of everyday life to take its toll on us. Over time we seem to lose that belief in what we do and say, while peace and happiness appear to slip away. Then the next thing you know you may be drifting in that state of mind for years, without ever realizing it.

I can see despair in many of the faces I speak with in everyday life. You must look at life as your friend.

We all go through difficult times in our lives. Yet I speak with many people that have been in a certain mindset for a long time. I try to comfort them by telling them there will be times when we cannot control certain circumstances that take place in our life. However, you can control how you will respond to those situations. I know it can be hard at times, but what else can we do?

We must try our best to move forward and gain the best life possible. Once you accept the situation your life will begin to take on a new meaning as you further advance your life.

By changing your perception of life it will affect everything you do and say. You will find that whatever you want to do will be easier to achieve than before. Once you perceive life and this world in a positive way then peace and happiness will seek their way into your life. Then whatever activities you once enjoyed will become fun once again. From time to time, I speak with people and see many with sad faces. I wonder if they may be in a difficult situation themselves just as I was. I wonder has their world closed in on them.

Seek the positive reinforcement and affirmations that I speak of here in my story. Use the other tools I speak of that life provided me also. Surround yourself with positive people and positive stories to read. I know through my own recovery I found it difficult at times. Yet when I applied these principles and tools, I saw positive change begin. I also began to see positive people come into my life more and more. It appeared as if I moved to a new and different level with life. I know believing serenity is possible and by doing this your life could turn around in a rather short time. Stay consistent and you too can see change.

Your days will become brighter and happiness will find its way into your life. I believe the energy in this universe works that way. Just start with a little at a time. Your view of life or just about everything you encounter may begin to alter. I know these principles worked for me, and given time, I believe it is possible they will work for you too. Remember to say the affirmations I mention here each day and seek serenity. It will find its way into your life.

Anthony J Rockweiler

Chapter 7

Surviving

As I look back, I realize that as difficult as it was to survive the accident it would prove to be the easiest part. It became clear to me early on that surviving over time would be a much different story. With so many injuries and the duration of time they would last they took a tremendous toll on me.

The situation overwhelmed me and drew me into a vicious cycle that I could not seem to get out of. It drew me farther inward into my mind each day. The psychological suffering alone day after day would test my belief system and faith beyond what I could imagine. At times I had no clue what was going to happen or take place. Coping over the long haul would be another test. With four out of five of my human senses diminished because of this ordeal, I found myself in an odd place for the first time in my life. You may not realize how much you depend on your senses until you find yourself in a situation like this. I could never imagine the path I found myself on, but there I was. Believe me it would not be easy to find my way back.

As I reflect back on the situation I can recall early on how my instincts told me to sleep so I could cope and adapt. The first year of therapy would wear a healthy person down. There were days when I felt like I could not go on. That is when I found myself standing on what I called the edge of reality, clinging to life.

There were also times when I was extremely afraid and I wondered if I was going to make that turn or not. I began questioning myself on many occasions as time passed. The suffering was relentless. When I look back now I realize those were the days when a force much greater than myself carried me. There were periods when I felt lost and isolated. Those days seemed so empty and filled with so much sadness. I learned a great deal about the life I wanted to live on those empty days. A powerful force drove me to improve even when there were days when I felt I could not go any further. There were also periods where I just sat in fear not knowing if I would regain my life back or not. It took me a long time before I gained control over the situation. The injuries drove me inward into my mind to a place where I had never been before. It appeared as if I was never going to get out of that cycle. The tinnitus drove me even farther inward and would not let up. It lasted such a long time and it scared me knowing that I could not escape that condition or turn it off.

As the uncertainty grew, I continued to meditate and go further into my mind for the answers.

As I followed that pathway deep into my mind it would lead me to a special place where healing and my view of this world would change.

What I believed to be the Creator would save my life allowing me to move forward and realize who holds, "The Power of Life". I was meditating daily for about three years before I was able to find this place and come back with a different perception of life. That different perception or "the power of life" would allow me to free myself of the mindset I was in for so long. I would go through a process where a recreation of myself would begin to take place. I always knew the human mind was capable of performing fascinating tasks. Little did I know that I would have to rely on it at such a deep level and at a critical time in my life? The way my life changed was unbelievable and remarkable at the same time. My view of life and this universe would never be the same again. I knew a powerful force that governs all of creation allowed me to come away with my life and a miracle of my own. That's the only way I could explain it. It would be the miracle of belief. I believe that powerful force was the Creator working through my spirit to heal and recreate me in many ways. I never experienced anything like that before. I went deep into my mind searching for answers in order to survive and found where life would reside. As a result, something mystical would take place that day as I returned with the miracle of life.

Because of this ordeal, I see the universe in a different way than before. I see and view stress, and pressure in a much different way also. I was the kind of person who could deal with stress and pressure well before the accident happened. Yet this was a completely different situation. The constant pain and psychological suffering over time became a critical factor in surviving. I wondered if I could hang on long enough to make it through. That became another powerful question for me to answer.

One doctor told me that everyone has a breaking point. As I look back on the situation I can only imagine how close I was to my breaking point on many occasions. I am humbled by knowing that God guided me out of a dark place and granted me the miracle of life.

I was trying to eradicate every condition I was dealing with. There came a time when I realized that may not be possible. I began to accept and see the conditions I had left in a different way. I can see how the Creator sculptured and molded me with love and compassion into the person I am now. I will never forget that. I realized the Creator reached out to me at a time when all seemed lost and I created a bond with life that I otherwise would not have had.

There were many days where I just felt broken. I

remember as time went on each day became a test of endurance and survival more and more.

Accepting and adapting became critical at that time. I realized that is when the Creator was with me the most. It was then when I connected with life on another level that allowed me to move forward again in a productive way. Many of my problems were still there, but something changed that day. The Creator gave me the hope and strength to move forward molding me along the way.

Something I could not explain took place that day. Something I believe you might not witness unless all traditional methods of medicine and healing fail. Then when you find yourself in a dire state knowing the end could be near. Your options have run out. Your belief has to be so strong that something will change.

You need a miracle. You need something you did not have before. You must rely on your bond with the Creator alone for survival. It is just you and life. Again I realized that no one else was coming for me. This is it. I exhausted all means.

Then something took place one day that would alter the way I see this world by the one who holds, "The Power of Life".

Looking back I can see there were times when I thought time was running out on me. Making that turn at that particular time became critical in order for me to survive. This universe must have known just how fragile I was at that precise time. Something mysterious would take place as I made that mystical turn. Molding of my old traits with my new ones in order to become a new person would be a tricky process. Yet as the process unfolded I was able to accept and love the man I would become. This would allow me to move forward once again with my life. When this ordeal first happened it appeared as if a tornado just passed through my mind. Therefore, it would take me some time to organize the turmoil I was in for so long. I thank God that I hung on and made it through such a rough period in my life. This process humbled me and I came away learning a great deal about this universe, life, and myself. It took me a long time and a great deal of patience before I could gain some type of relief. There were so many things happening at once. I am not sure if I would be alive today if things would not have went the way they did.

I know part of improving was telling people I was doing okay when I was not.
They would ask, "How are you?" and I would say, "I'm doing well." However, that was one of the hardest things to do, but I did it every day until I finally started to believe it myself. By doing so I began to adapt to my situation a little easier as each day passed. Because of that my conditions began to improve and I began to find myself in a peaceful place more and more.

That repetitive thinking process I was doing would help save my life instead of destroying it. What prepares you for an ordeal like this? Not a whole lot I can tell you that. I also realized that period was the loneliest time of my life. I also share my story to let people know these feelings of loneliness and isolation can pass. I made it through this difficult time and you can too.

I know when I was going through these times of desperation and despair it molded me into who I am today. I returned with something I was not aware of at first. These experiences from this ordeal would be the gifts that would determine how I wanted to live my life. Life would mold and sculpture me into what it wanted and not necessary into what I wanted.

At the time I did not know anyone else that suffered an injury like the one I was dealing with. There was so much confusion running through my mind from day to day. This left me feeling even more alone. At first I had no idea if I could make it back to be anything close to the person I was before. Even though I found myself confused on many occasions I still pushed forward each day. Something compelled me to forge ahead not knowing what the outcome would be. That is how I knew a force much greater than man carried me.

In the early stages of the accident some people stayed away from me for some reason or another. I was not quite sure if it was out of fear or perhaps they had no idea what to say to me.

At other times the isolation made me feel as though I had some contagious disease you could catch. I got the feeling some people kept their distance from me because they were afraid themselves. This is what my instincts told me. Your instincts are invaluable. As I said before, it was just something I felt deep inside and something I could not explain. Those days and nights seemed extra lonely for me, but I understand. I believe they could see for themselves that a tragedy like this could possibly pass through anyone's life, including their own. Staying away from me perhaps was a way people could distance themselves from the reality that bad things can happen to good people. I know I just got an inert feeling deep inside which gave me these feelings I never experienced before. I think people keeping their distance had a lot to do with fear. I struggled through so many different and new emotions at the time and really did not dwell on this particular phenomenon. As I improved the feeling of isolation also decreased improving my connection with life and people once again.

After years of therapy and going through this ordeal life has taught me so much about myself. I have come to a place where I am more comfortable today with myself than I ever before. I am happy with the outcome and I remain humble, by the process. It was not easy. I still live with some of the residual effects. Yet I love who I am more than ever. I was able to overcome a hopeless situation and return to a productive life once again. As a result, I acquired a new perception of this world along the way.

As my story unfolded I never gave up hope or the belief that something greater than myself would step in. I was able to cling on to life and as a result everything changed. I would like to say this: be the best you can be each day. Have a strong belief in yourself, and an even greater belief, in a much greater power. You can come back from what may appear to be a hopeless event and live a fulfilling and happy life. I am living proof of that.

Returning to exercising was another way of finding my way back to something I once loved. I would wonder many days if I could ever return to exercising and still find it fulfilling. Now I rely more on my diet along with science and supplements to create a healthy physique. I also depend on meditation and rest more than ever. I am somewhat limited by the effects of what happen so now I rely on science and nutrition more than before.

After finding peace once again it led me back to the things I once enjoyed. There are days I sit back and look at the overall picture and see the mystique surrounding it. It shows that your mind is capable of creating incredible events even though you may not believe so.

The human mind and body are unbelievable gifts. Together they make a phenomenal combination. I know this much, I came back from an event that seemed impossible to do. I thank God for that. By using positive words and positive thoughts I was able to influence the outcome. I remain grateful and humble. Do and be something greater than yourself. Life should be about giving not taking.

As I try to live by this notion it seems to bring a rewarding feeling to my life.
I know I look at life along with this world through a different pair of eyes now. A tragedy does not need to pass through your life to do the things I am suggesting. Inundate yourself with positive thoughts and positive feelings as much as you can. Read positive material and

find positive people to associate yourself with as you reach for a better life. If you find the people in your life are always talking negative than I would seek a new circle of friends. I am not saying leave them behind. If they see your life begin to improve then perhaps they will follow you to a better life. Remember, positive people may experience setbacks, but many consider them opportunities to learn. Love yourself and live each day with a passion and the principles of the universe will do the rest.

Chapter 8

Forgiveness for Myself

When I think about this word—forgiveness—
I wonder about many things. I viewed myself for the
most part as a bright fellow and confident in what I did
and said. Therefore, when I found myself in this
situation, I felt this sense of letting myself down, or
failing myself in some way. It made me feel like I
should have known something or protected myself in
some way or another. When in reality, I know there
was nothing I could have done. Regardless, I still felt
this sense of failing myself. I was often trying to come
to terms with these feelings along with the other
conditions I was dealing with. I kept going over the
course of events in my mind looking for something I
could have done to change the outcome.

I could see there was nothing that I could have done
that would have altered the situation. Yet, I just kept
looking until I finally faced the fact that the accident
just happened.

Only later down the road I would find out to some degree what I believe took place that day.

Meanwhile, I kept saying, "Forgive yourself forgive yourself. It will be okay. Just forgive yourself." Then I started to look at the word forgiveness. What happens when you forgive? What does it mean and what takes place? For me I had to forgive the man that went to work that Monday morning, so the man I would become could move forward. I struggled with this for a long time until I let go of the man I once was, and came to understand the man I would become. It was as if I knew that man well, but I was no longer that man in so many ways. I sat and cried many days over losing myself and walking away. So coming to know and understand the new feelings I had, in conjunction with the old ones would take me some time.

Letting go so I could find that place in the middle where forgiveness could start meant so much to me. Experiencing some of these new feelings would be somewhat of an odd feeling in itself. At times, it was frustrating. I found myself annoyed many times on different occasions. I know forgiving, understanding, and adapting became a tricky process. Adapting meant merging the two personalities together, finding peace, and feeling complete once again. Then the process of forgiving could start to take place and allow me to move forward in a positive way.

With that in mine it would allow the merging process to take place.

I began to see the two different people, the man I was and the man I had become and I began putting little pieces of both of them together with each passing day. Knowing the person I once was and learning to adapt to the person I had become was a little easier as time passed.

I could see the old me standing on the side in my mind, but I was no longer that person. I knew I would have to leave him behind as I looked back and waved goodbye. That was hard as I had tears in my eyes.

As I said before, none of us are who we were yesterday. I believe something happens to each one of us on a daily basis that changes who we are in some way or another. Our ability to experience, learn, forgive and move forward allows us to grow and advance to a new level in life.

For me, it was difficult until the day finally arrived when I let go and found forgiveness for myself. I walked away and began to love myself all over again, which was a tremendous blessing. As a result, I am more comfortable with who I am now than ever before. As I just said this, I just waved good-bye to the man I once was in my mind and walked away. I began to love life with a passion and I found peace once again. This process reminded me of when I was a young boy and would piece cars together, building and creating something completely new. It would be a completely different car. Out of that creation a whole new vehicle would surface. It would be a sleeker, faster and better looking car. Taking pieces of different objects in my youth like automobiles to create something new appeared to be a blueprint to my life and my future. My background and my resourcefulness throughout my life couldn't have a surface at a more precise and important time allowing me to my recover my life once again.

Those tools or resources would find their way back into my life at thirty-six to create the ultimate project, "Myself."

However, it was not always that way. It took me some time, but I made it through what I call the "passage". It was a narrow corridor with life on one side and desperation on the other. I spent years in that corridor, clinging to life, wondering, "Who am I", and will I make it back?" I would learn many things about life and about myself in this process. Through that understanding I hope you live each day in a passionate way. I believe we all have an ability connect to this universe on a spiritual level, and to one another.

Yet, I feel we do not use this resource enough. It feels like a metaphysical process is taking place. The connection we have, I believe, is part of our creation. I realized that I forced myself to tap into my mind in ways I did not understand at the time. As a result, it gave me a chance to survive. Tapping into that resource would give me a chance to accept many things including the man I would become.

For me, I came to an understanding that none of us are who we were yesterday. That brought me some comfort and helped me adapt to my own situation. In my case the change was rather instant.

I went to work one man and came home another, yet I still found that passion for life and living once again. I hope you become more comfortable with who you are and how you can live life with that passion every day.

Again taking pieces of the man I was and instilling new traits and experiences from what I learned allowed me to rebuild a new life for myself. Once again, as I reflect back it reminded me of when I was young building automobiles. It would allow me to piece different automobiles together and make it something I could really be proud of when I finished. As I look at myself I can see how that same process was beginning to unfold. It was just a more intricate and unique way in order to restore myself to a new and higher level of awareness with a new life.

Accepting myself for the person I would become was another major part of the healing process. It allowed me to move forward and find happiness and peace. Some of my emotions now I measure on a different scale than before. I also see life in a different way than I did before. I wanted to have that strong bond with life once again. Therefore, I know it is possible that each one of us can gain or regain that bond with life once again. Our situations may be different. We all suffer from something or another, but our outcome can be the same. Here in my story I found happiness, peace, and harmony with life once again. Some emotions I thought were gone forever, but that was not the case.

From where I was at it appeared as if there was no

return. Once again, never give up hope and pursue happiness in life. Believe all things are possible by seeking a greater power, greater than yourself and you too can feel "The Power of Life".

In return, the Creator will give you all the love and guidance you need.

Never give up on yourself. We will all find ourselves in situations that may seem hopeless or difficult to overcome. I know each day brings something new, a new beginning. Believe that your circumstances can improve, and a greater power will improve them. Finding peace and happiness may be closer and easier than you think. Life gave me the peace and happiness I was looking for, and in return, peace and happiness restored my life. To me, there is no greater teacher than your life experiences. I followed my instincts and I listened, and did what my spirit asked of me. I made it back from some extreme and difficult times and I know you can too. Make a commitment to yourself every day when you wake up. It may sound minor, but it can be more powerful than one can imagine. Positive thinking is a powerful force. It cannot only change you, but it can change the way you see the world.

That type of thinking brought a power I never experienced before. You may also begin to see people and life in a different way than you did before

Positive thinking can also change the people around you. Every day I meet people who come into my life carrying a message meant only for me and changing my life in some way. I often have people tell me, "I wish I could meet wonderful people every day." I tell them, "You are meeting wonderful people every day. It is your perception of them that must change. When that changes you will begin to see what I'm talking about."

Living life is about how you perceive life itself. Your perception of life will make a huge difference in determining your quality of life. Try your best to remain positive.

Enjoyment will find its way back into your life much quicker than you think. You must make the first move. Life is always waiting and reaching out to you each day. I know in my case that it was difficult at first to reach out. I had to relearn so many things all over again. Remain consistent and you will find that with each passing day you will begin to see a change. It may be small at first. Do not get frustrated. Be patient. Over the course of time, you too may begin to start seeing things around you in a different way. You will find yourself smiling and laughing more each day along the way. The things you once enjoyed will begin to bring you pleasure and happiness again. It is possible. Your days can become less stressful, and happiness will begin to fill the void.

My affirmations are with me on a subconscious level. They have become an integrated part of my mind. Saying my affirmations is no longer necessary at this point. They are part of my everyday life. They are part of me now; I am not part of them. These affirmations are a constant reminder of just how precious my quality of life is to me. They allowed many things to take place including forgiveness.

Once I allowed forgiveness to take place I began to deal with the fear and uncertainty in a better way. For most of my life I considered myself a confident person. Yet, in a split second that confidence slipped away from me and in a flash that man was gone. I found myself uncertain about everything. At that point it appeared as if I had no control over my life and the accident was just pulling me along for the ride. I pushed forward daily for some type of improvement in the quality of my life. That became such an important issue in my rehabilitation. To this day I cherish my quality of life with all my heart. I remind myself each day just how lucky I am to be alive. Moving forward may have been slow, but at least I was moving in the right direction. Sorting through and organizing so many issues at once took me some time, but there was no other way. I can remember the sheer extent of it all and how dealing with it over time was difficult.

Merging two people in order to find a new identity would take me some time and patience. It was a challenge to merge them, but an even bigger challenge to find peace and happiness once again. When I look back, now I realize just how lucky I was in doing so. I would need to take control and find an identity for myself.

It would prove to be a challenging process. There also seemed to be a mystery that surrounded me from day to day. I was not sure what the outcome would be. There are so many intricate pieces to you and your personality. You have to take into account your environment along with your life experiences. Believe me, it can be a delicate and daunting task.

With my emotions and other conditions running away, it became a fragile process. Finding acceptance became tricky. There were so many pieces of the puzzle to assemble and forgiveness was one of them. I feel more comfortable with myself today than ever before. I remain humble knowing that a greater force restored my life, and the darkness lifted as I returned to a new world. I now have an understanding of life that I would not otherwise have. In the process, I would learn a great deal about my connection with the Creator and about myself. I discovered how awesome the universe that we live in could be. At the time, finding peace and acceptance became instrumental in order for me to survive. There was just so much going on in the first couple of years and I had no idea where to turn. As a result it took some time before the pieces would come together.

I could sense the end of the road was near. There was nowhere to go and I felt as if time was running out on me. I continued to meditate hoping something would change. I was desperate and needed to find a way out of the situation I found myself in for so long.

Then one day something would happen that would change the course of everything.

I found myself led out of a dark place and back into a different world. There a new life would be waiting for me. I believe the Creator would grant me the gift of life, a miracle. I generated my own miracle by believing it was possible. I will never forget that feeling or that day. There were many times over the course of my life that I hurt myself in some way or another, but it was nothing like this. The severity of the injuries was crushing and powerful. I know the constant pressure was relentless. It drove me inward almost instantly. Once that happened, I could not get out of that cycle. It was something I never experienced before. Not knowing what was going to happen became the most frightening part. I know the situation appeared to engulf me right away. That is why it became so important for me to make a turn in the right direction and as soon as possible.

Forgiveness was in the midst of this process and yet another aspect of my recovery. Forgiveness played an important role in allowing me to move forward. Because of the forgiveness process I find myself able to forgive much easier than I did before. I just overlook many situations or pay no attention to them at all. Sometimes when I see pain in someone's eyes for some reason I think of forgiveness. For me, in this process the two appeared related. It seems like every day I speak with someone who is not having a good day. I try to bring some form of happiness and comfort into their life by speaking with them and sharing my story. I try to bring hope into their life, letting them see they are never alone. I share my perspective of life that many may not have heard. It seems to bring a smile to their face.

Many times when I leave after speaking with them, I can see the difference in their eyes already.

Chapter 9

Your Quality Of Life

I can see there were forces at work that under normal conditions I would have never been aware of. If this had not taken place, I would have not been able to see something incredible about this universe. The view of humanity I had in this type of ordeal was something I will never forget. It gives you a view of life that you may otherwise never see. When you are in a fight for your survival, the meaning of life and being human take on new meanings. You begin to realize there is something much greater at work than you were aware of before. When desperation sets in and you realize you may not make it back, you will know exactly what I mean. There is no outside help. You realize there is no one coming for you. You must rely on a belief that something can or will change. Your life depends on it.

I remain grateful for the outcome. When you lose your identity, but you are still alive, it is a strange feeling. The man that fell on that Monday morning in May lost a dear friend.

I searched for a new identity. I knew who I was, but I thought who am I now? Life as I knew it became much different in those days. That reality reshaped and sculptured me into what I needed to be, not necessary want I wanted to be. Redefining the man I became through this ordeal was a much larger task than one may think or imagine. In the end, you must love the person you have become. You realize there is a greater force at work every day that you may not be aware of setting everything into motion. That reality came into play. As different aspects of my personality began to fall in place, I was able to find that love for myself once again. At first, it was not easy. In the early stages of this process I needed tools that were not available to me at the time of the accident.

Through this journey these tools became available which led me to the gift of life, and a miracle. I would go into this ordeal one man, and in the end, I would become another, recreated in many ways. Afterwards, I was able to go on and live in peace and happiness, which is something we all seek. That peace and happiness is a place in our mind, it is something that we create and it is where you will find serenity. My belief would lead me to a meeting that would alter my life and set my feet on an unbelievable path back to a new world. I believe it begins with having a bond with life and being content and happy with just being alive. I hear people say there are so many things they cannot control. Yet, you can make a decision today to wake up tomorrow and be happy.

Realize that decision is a gift and by realizing that you can avoid one tragedy. Make a decision today to see life and view it in a positive way. That is within your power. Just use the tools I share with you in my story.

There are two ways to live your life, one as if nothing is a miracle, and one as if everything is. Stand in awe of life itself, and the creation of it. Life is about giving, not taking. I believe that you should give to life and expect nothing in return. If you try this, you just may see changes in your own life that perhaps you may not have noticed before. I believe it is one of principles of this universe. The energy you put out is the energy you will receive. To me, that is how you balance your life. I believe that if you view the world in a good way, good things will come into your life. I often say expect good things to happen to you and they will. You may begin to see people and events in your life change and shift as well. You see, life does not need to change. Perhaps the way we see or view life may need to change, but not life itself.

Change your perception of life and the world you live in and then everything begins to take on a new meaning. You may think life changed, but that is not the case. The things around you are the same. Just give the process some time and allow it to unfold. You may begin to feel like you and life are more in harmony than you did before. Life may seem to flow in a more natural state making you feel more alive than ever before. Then you may begin to view the world in a different way. I love helping people get the best quality of life possible for themselves. When I share my view of life, it seems to give them a different view of living than they had before. The words I use and the view of life I have now appear to be something many people have not heard before.

Many times, it may be the words I say or the passion I use to express them. Afterwards, people may say,

"You know, I never thought about it that way!

You just gave me an answer to a problem I'm facing." Always remember, there is power in your words and in the tone of your voice. Words are powerful tools not only in your life but also in the life of everyone you meet throughout your day.

I realized some of the decisions I had to make throughout this ordeal to save my life were difficult. I had to rely and trust my instincts more than ever, even with my five human senses altered, making things even more confusing for me. Once that happened, I had to rely on resources built into my mind like never before. Our mind is performing tasks all day long that we are not even aware of until you find yourself in a situation like this. My world did not slow down that day, it came to a complete stop. So for me it was amazing how other resources just stepped in and began helping. Certain areas of your mind come to assist you in situations like this. That was fascinating to witness.

Looking back I can see how it all came together to

help bring me out of that dark place and back to pursuing the life I wanted. I can see how I listened and followed a path that life laid out for me, through my power of belief. Western medicine did a phenomenal job, but I was still devastated years down the road. I knew my options were running out and it became clear to me that my belief would need to be stronger than ever. I knew my survival would depend on it.

Therefore, each day while meditating, I reinforced that belief until something changed. I am thankful I made that turn when I did and the greatest force in the universe stepped in knowing how fragile I was. I knew time was running out on me. I had no idea where to turn and I was still suffering with many physical and emotional conditions.

Traditional medicine did all it could for me, but I was still feeling alone and isolated. I know this much, I am glad things changed when they did; otherwise I am not sure what would have happen. I was fragile, broken, and still overcome by my circumstances.

As my life begin to turn around, I would go back out into the world and begin meeting some extraordinary people. I know this much, people started coming into my life out of nowhere at that particular time. It was as if a completely new world was opening up for me.

Words became such a powerful tool in this process. For me words took on a completely new meaning, playing such an important role in building a new life for myself. Using words and reinforcing positive affirmations would return my life back to me. Words would return my self-esteem, my self-image and my self-confidence to me once again. Three very important tools as I returned to a new life and new world.

When I meet people, I find myself sharing my story and my thoughts on positive thinking. I find myself asking them, "Do you have any negative people around you that are in your life?" I cannot remember one of them saying no. If people are derogating you or treating you in a negative way, I see that as an attack on your character. I cannot see how you can thrive in that environment. You cannot allow someone to attack your character. That is the only thing you have in life. When you strip everything else away, the only thing remaining is the core of you.

They can take material possessions from you, but never let someone take away your character. It is who you are.
If people cannot respect you, then move away from them until they learn how. Then they can build a positive relationship with you. By respecting you, they earn the right to be in your life again. You set boundaries on what you will, and will not accept.

I see many people that seem to have a sad look on their face. Remember, our life has a way of revealing itself on our face. I speak with people quite a bit about positive thinking and building a bond with life. You can find happiness in just being alive. You want to view life with that perspective. Then you can go on to live the best quality of life possible. Some may believe that life revolves around money or possessions but it does not. Life revolves around finding true happiness and peace. Believe things can change and they will.

As your bond with life strengthens, your bond with people will strengthen also. I do not believe it is the other way around. You cannot let negative thoughts control your mind and tarnish your thinking.

Build your bond with life and accept it for the gift that it is supposed to be. Believe in yourself and you will see positive energy come into your everyday world. Say positive things to yourself and think positive. Tell life how much you love it each day. You will start to see the negative things around you beginning to diminish. Do not be surprised if you begin to see the world in a different way than you did before.

Remember, you write the script to your own life. No one else does. If you find yourself surrounded by nothing but negative comments, it will begin to bring you down. You need to put yourself in a different environment.

Begin looking for positive people to surround yourself with and watch how they speak and carry themselves. Then watch how your life changes. Remember, happiness and peace comes from within. Get yourself in an environment where you will find support. I know working on oneself can be somewhat of a challenge. I can recall in rehab early on in my own situation when speaking with the doctor about certain things in my life. It seemed a little odd at first, yet as time went on, I could see how I gained insight into my own life. I gained a view of myself along with my environment that set me free. It helped me in so many areas of my life and I consider myself fortunate. I began to look at my life in a different way. I speak more open than I did before. I also have an understanding of not only my past, but also my future.

You must believe you are capable of doing things and you will. You must believe you can find happiness and you will. Even when I was a young boy I remember believing in what I did and said. When I was young, I had the ability to take things apart and fix them. I just had a belief that I could do it. I had no one to show me how to disassemble an automobile. I just did it knowing I could and that is how I approached most things in my early life and still to this day. Through belief you can create a place of happiness in your mind just as I did.

I can remember as a young boy going outside on a cool evening at night and looking up into the sky.

It gave me such an awesome feeling and I realized how lucky I was to be alive. The world was so beautiful to me and I viewed it in an amazing way.

It appeared so majestic. The things I thought of at nine and ten were much differently than other young people or people in general. I had so many questions about so many things. Who am I, where did I come from, and can I heal myself. When will we be able to speak without words and use a different form of communication? Where did the Universe come from? Who and where is the Creator. Where is the beginning of the universe? It was just a lot of questions for a young boy who thought on a deeper level. Sometimes I look in the mirror and my eyes can still see that young boy even though time has passed. I recall having a passion for living life even then. I hope I never lose that little boy in me. I know throughout my life I had people say to me, there is something different about you. Have you ever felt that way? I would reply yes. When I was young growing into a man I had this feeling I would change the world in some way or another. However, I thought every young person did.

For me, when that day in May came, the world I once knew would no longer be the world I remembered. When I lost my self-confidence, my self-esteem, and my self-image, all in a flash, it was an odd feeling. Even now when I look back, I can see how far I have come to be where I am today. It is truly remarkable.

For instance, words were difficult to speak and articulate in order to form a sentence. Now I love to talk. I wondered if I would be able to write again and here I am, sharing my story with you. I found that love for myself all over again. I believe in myself once again, but at one point, I thought that might be gone forever. I see many miracles within my own miracle of survival here in my story even when I read it.

I stand in awe knowing I came back from something I should not have and I know you can too. Look for the many miracles within my story.

Let your mind wander and it will take you to places where you once thought impossible. Let your imagination be your guide and you will overcome hurdles you once thought were impossible also. You have the ability to control your thoughts each day. You can make that decision today and say, "I am going to be happy tomorrow." No one can take that from you. You can create your world by thought. Remember you think what you become and become what you think. I thought and created the world I wanted to come back to. I know it is possible because I did it, and you can too.

Each day say these words: "I want to have a passion for life every day." They may seem like simple words, but do not be surprised when you begin to see people come into your life you did not see before. Perhaps you may realize that some of them were there all along. These people may bring something that can improve your life in significant ways. Just remain open-minded, and by doing so you allow things to come into your life. Believe that your life will improve each day and it will. You can create the world you live in. I did.

When you look back on your life, I bet you can recall situations you were in and thought at the time you had no way out. You may have said to yourself, "I don't have the money, the talent or the experience. The right people are not in my life." Whatever you may have thought, try to remember that you found a way to get through it. Believe there is a way, and the way will come to you. That seems to be another principle of life.

Think about good people coming into your life, and they have a way of appearing right before your eyes.

Believe in your talent and it will grow and manifest in ways you never imagined. Life has always been by your side. Just call upon it and watch your world change in ways you never dreamed possible.

Find that belief in yourself. Each day reinforce positive thoughts such as, "I am radiant, bright, full of energy, and love life." Tell yourself you love who you are. Awaken yourself to the reality of change. Then you can see your world move in a direction that is full of unbelievable love and happiness. Your reality becomes what you think it is. So believe the world is a wonderful place and you will create that wonderful world for yourself. When you get up in the morning, remember that every day is fun and see it as a new adventure or new beginning.

You will begin to see how you have the power to change things around you and influence things in your life. At times, I hear people say to me, "The people I work with have bad attitudes." Well, that may be true. You may be the one person who can change their lives. Look at it this way. You have more power than you think. Believe in yourself and carry yourself a certain way. Remember, you alone can change the world around you. Do not wait for something good to happen. Create something good. It can start with a simple thought. That is all it may take. Perhaps it could begin with just a simple smile. The effects of that gesture could expand out reaching and changing the course of many lives and making many friends.

You yourself hold that power and when used daily you can single-handedly change lives. By doing so, you too can witness "the power of life". I believe when you help people you not only empower them but also empower yourself advancing yourself to a new level of awareness in life. It is a feeling that only life can give you.

I was always a big dreamer. I have been that way since I was a kid and when this bump in the road came along it changed all of that in an instant. Once again, it shows you just what the power of belief can do. I can remember before this accident happened believing in myself and believing there had to be a greater power. Here in my story, my belief would lead me to a miracle that would save my life and recreate me. Afterwards, life would set my feet on an unbelievable journey, allowing me to see this world in a unique way. When I look back on my recovery and where I came from, it still has a profound effect on me. I was not supposed to return. So, if you want a better life, create that life by believing so, just as I did. Then your reality will come to you. When people see you applying yourself, it has a way of drawing good things into your life. It is another way of improving your quality of life.

As you focus on a better life, a better life will come to you. You must think on those terms. You do not need a tragedy or series of events to take place in order to change your quality of living. That may never happen. You can change it by influencing your thinking, and your perception of life will begin to alter. Start perceiving life and people in a different way and a completely new world can open up for you too.

I believe positive change begins with each one of us and ripples outward. It also leaves a path of happiness and peace that is waiting for each one of us. I challenge you, try it today and watch how the world around you begins to change. It liberated me and brought me back to a new and even better world.

With those words "act as if" you can create a better you, and in return, you will create a belief unlike before. The tranquility you feel will allow you to evolve to a new level.

I also believe if you want a better life, than remember, there is a greater power you can reach out to for help.

Then a better world and a gratifying life will find its way to you.

You can also "act as if" you have what you want—happiness. By acting as if you are happy, you will begin to see happiness flowing into your life. "Act as if "life is amazing, and you will find amazement in your own life and the world around you. "Act as if" this world is fascinating, and it will set your feet on a fascinating journey meant only for you.

Cherish every day you are alive. Just be happy about living life each day, and life will do the rest. Remember that we own nothing—cars, houses, or belongings. These objects were here when we came, and they will be here when we are gone. All we are doing is borrowing them. We can get peace and happiness through our bond with a greater power and our perception of life. When life strips everything away from you, all you have is what is inside of you. I am not perfect by any means; I am just a human being. I try to live by a certain code and certain belief, because that is all I have.

Chapter 10

The Power We All Possess

As I wind down this final chapter, I remain humble by this experience and see life as a precious gift. I hope I never lose sight of that truth. I want to live my life as if each day is a new beginning. I am thankful for the wisdom and knowledge that I obtained throughout this process. I am lucky. You can look at something like this in two ways. One as a tragedy, or two, that I was lead to "The Power of Life" on a spiritual journey that advanced me to another level. I am thankful for the outcome and choose to see this journey in a positive way. I know there is a greater power that will always be by my side, teaching me new experiences along the way. Each day I learn something new about this universe and something new and different about myself. I feel so fortunate that everything came together the way that it did. I was able to receive the gift of life, my own miracle. I am grateful and lucky at the same time.

Never give up hope. For me, when all means seemed exhausted, and all hope appeared gone, I would rise out of the ashes of despair. My life altered and restored through a remarkable process. You too can get the same results. Remain positive and believe things can change. Believe your quality of life can and will change. Believe a greater power can and will step in, and alter your life. My perception of many things changed in a remarkable way, and all in a single moment. The way I see life now changed forever.

Meeting the people I have through this journey would also prove to be another precious gift.

Remember to wake up each morning and embrace life for the gift that it is. Look to advance your life and quality of life by the choices you make. Be happy about going out into the world and changing someone's life in a positive way. Remember, just a smile can have a huge impact on someone's day. You never know what that person may be going through at that particular time in their life. That smile may send a sign to them that people do care. One person can change lives.

I believe many of us never realize the role we play in the lives of other people, from day to day. Even the way you say a particular sentence to someone can have a huge impact in his or her life. Two people can say the same sentence to someone, yet they can come away with two different meanings. Perhaps it may be the person's tone of voice or the speed and sensitivity in which they convey their message. In rehab, I paid close attention when using words once again, and came away realizing the true power in them.

They appeared to have a new meaning, and took on a unique and different role. I realized words were not just words but another powerful tool that I could use in my life. The power we hold in our words has the ability to enhance or derogate someone's life. We have the ability to bring more sorrow or more happiness into someone's world. I consider that a powerful force at work considering you and I hold that ability each day. Think about this, you have the ability to mold someone's life by using simple words.

The power of the human mind would prove to be another incredible tool that I used to recover my life. Calling on my mind was like calling on someone else for help. So many things became available to me as a result of going within my mind. It appeared as if a new world opened preparing a new life for me. What would it be like if we were able to use our mind at an early age, the way I was able to do here? What would our life be like?

In this country, I believe we do not understand how to interact with our mind in that manner. I remember as a young boy always challenging my mind for an answer. I also wondered, what is the meaning of life and where do I go from here? I knew the human mind was remarkable, but I also knew there was something much greater than mankind. I knew there had to be a higher force or Creator. I believe when we tap into our mind in a certain way, then we can become closer to the Creator. I believe our mind is set up that way. I believe this universe creates an energy that we can tap into and have some influence in the process. For me, I would need to call on my mind in way I never dreamed possible.

As a result it led me down a path that was unknown and fascinating. How I interacted with my mind and the resources that became available to me I will never forget. Through my belief process I was able to tap into a place in my mind and it would alter the way I see this world. When I did, everything would change that day and I would come back with the miracle of life.

I remember it was somewhere around the fifth year mark after the accident. I was spending a great deal of time each day meditating. Around that time, a force much greater than man would step in and my perception of this world would change. I could feel throughout this process as if I was being re-created. Afterwards, my perception of life and my circumstances would take on a different meaning. I began to see my vocabulary and my ability to articulate sentences beginning to improve. I also began to see the power of words in a different way than I did before. I began to see the way I used words in a different manner, along with the way people responded to them. I could also see my self-esteem beginning to rise as it became another vital part of my recovery. That is when I began to realize how powerful and compelling words could be. So each day I would try to improve my vocabulary. As time passed and my vocabulary improved I began to feel comfortable using words. Then I found myself speaking with people a little more with each passing day. It was interesting how this process all played out. I believe there was a purpose for it at the time which I did not understand. I can recall in the early phase of the accident how I pushed myself out every day, even when I was afraid.

Fear tried to keep me locked inside as if I was some sort of prisoner, but I forced myself back out into the world. If I was going to get any quality of life I knew I had to go.

In those early days I was so afraid, but I overcame those fears to live life once again. Remember, you can too. At first, it was hard, but it got easier as time went on. My vocabulary improved as time passed, which also helped as I went back into the world. So composing words to articulate sentences would become important to me. They would unlock another major aspect of this process and free me like never before. This ordeal exposed me to so many new experiences and I am grateful for the outcome.

The tools I acquired throughout this journey still amaze me today. Words became my friend and another crucial tool that I will always remember. These "gifts" I call them, each played a vital role in returning my life to me and helping others along the way. I speak with people in a different way than I did before. It's funny when I think about it. Some people say to me, "You talk more than a woman," and I just have to laugh. I know the world I re-entered was not the world I left, but that was fine with me. I returned to a new world because of this journey. I left behind many things including the man that left for work that Monday morning in May. I had to come to terms with that and it was hard in the beginning, but I love the man I am now.

My new world came with many new experiences that lead me down a mystical road where a new life was waiting. I would have all the resources available for a new beginning. Remember here in my story you can do the same thing.

Believe in yourself and never forget the power of belief. It saved my life and altered my perception of this world forever. Remember you become what you think and think what you become. Think good things about yourself and believe your life will improve and it will.

Positive thoughts can bring positive energy and positive people into your life. I am living proof of that.

Then you too can see your life move in a positive direction. Reinforce positive affirmations to yourself and watch your life improve for the better. Know there is a higher power you can call on, and all you need to do is believe that change is possible. Believing can also bring the necessary tools into your life, just as it did for me.

Being resourceful is one of them. Resourcefulness is a tool we should learn in school at a young age. It can carry someone through many difficult situations in life.

I believe one of the first tools to instill into a young person is being resourceful. It can help instill a belief in someone which can offer other resources to benefit their life. I used it throughout my life and in this case to help as a survival skill. I know when I found myself in this particular situation, many resources came into play.

I know being resourceful was an asset that would lead me to many others tools that I would need. I will always be grateful for its use.

I believe the most important gift we have is "The Power of Belief" which is priceless. With the power of belief, you can orchestrate and bring the most important thing into your life. For example, here in my story, all in one day my world changed in a miraculous way and my life returned to me.

The miracle of belief took place, as a greater force would save my life.

Perceive life as your dear friend each day. Wake up each morning and say, "I love life and want a passion for living life each day." At first, you do not even need to believe it. The belief will come. Give yourself a little time and watch the world you live in change in a ways you could not imagine. Then the life you would like to have will seem to flow to you, rather than away from you. Life is not about what you own or can acquire, it is about how you perceive it. Love yourself for who you are. I think you will find that process alone amazing, along with the results.

Once something happens in our life the only thing we can do is learn from that experience. By learning and accepting that process it allows us to move forward and get the most out of life. I know when I did I began to see changes I never seen before. I bonded with life becoming its best friend all over again. This is another lesson I take away from this ordeal. Learning from this experience was a humbling process and one I will never forget. Now I have an exceptional bond and passion for living life once again. I love it more and more as each day passes.

Also, remember the role meditation played in my recovery. It can do the same for you. It led me out of darkness and to a place that saved my life.

Also remember, hope and happiness is all around you. Just reach out for them and believe you can obtain them. Through belief and positive reinforcement, the mind and body are capable of extraordinary things. When you couple that with the power of the Universe, then all things become possible.

I am living proof of that. Therefore, whatever circumstances you may find yourself in, you can overcome them just as I did. Do not give up hope, and do not give up on yourself.

Remember here in my story, I exhausted all means and I was desperate as I called out, "I need a miracle." Then one day everything changed and a meeting with destiny would determine my fate. "The Power of Life" would restore my life, as I returned with a miracle, the miracle of life. Also, remember, we all have the ability to call out and change our lives. The unbelievable Power of Belief, it transformed and recreated my life, and it can do the same for you. Never give up hope. The Creator of the universe is always there to help you.

I hope through my story you were able to gain some insight on acquiring the best quality of life you can. We should take nothing for granted. Take what life gives you and try your best to move forward, learning from each new experience. That is all we can do. If we hold on to bitterness and anger, it will only overshadow our chances of improving our quality of life.

"The Power of Life" is waiting; all you have to do is believe. Remarkable things can happen when you set belief into motion. You can even create a new world for yourself just I did here in my story. Remember life
is your friend, embrace it for the gift that it is. As I returned to this world, a new life awaited me and I will never forget that feeling.

Believe in yourself and that belief alone will open new doors for you and shed light on a new beginning.

Believe in yourself and watch your life change like never before just as mine did. Believe in something greater than yourself and watch things you thought were impossible, become possible. just as they did for me. I believed my way into saving my live and not giving up and I know you can too.

Now that this story is behind me it taught me so many valuable lessons. I recovered my life venturing out once again. I begin a new life in many ways. I also returned to bodybuilding thirteen years later and I still find it fun and fascinating. My perception of people and life has changed so much. Life became fun once again. I see obstacles now as something life is offering me to move to a higher level of awareness in this world.

28925089R00081

Made in the USA
Columbia, SC
26 October 2018